No Saloon in the Valley

No Saloon in the Valley

The Southern Strategy of Texas
Prohibitionists in the 1880s

James D. Ivy

Baylor
University
Press
Waco, TX 76798

Cover Photos:

"E.L. Dohoney": 13th Legislature portrait detail
Texas State Library and Archives Commission

Mrs. W. M. Baines, Houston resident and president of Eight Texas District of the Women's Christian Temperance Union, holds picture of Francis Willard, founder of W.C.T.U.
The UT Institute of Texan Cultures at San Antonio No. 0119-1
Courtesy of the San Antonio Light Collection

Copyright © 2003 by Baylor University Press
Waco, Texas, 76798
All Rights Reserved

Library of Congress Cataloging-in-Publication Data

Ivy, James D.
  No saloon in the valley : the southern strategy of Texas prohibitionists in the 1880s / James D. Ivy.
     p. cm.
Includes bibliographical references and index.
  ISBN 978-1-4813-1108-3 (hardcover : alk. paper)
  1. Prohibition--Texas--History. I. Title.

HV5090.T4I82 2003
363.4'1'09764--dc21
                              200215453

for Linda and the boys

Contents

Acknowledgments ix

Introduction: Southern Strategies 1

1 "The Lone Star State Surrenders to a Lone Woman":
  Frances Willard"s 1882 Texas Tour 7

2 "The Voice of the People is the Voice of God":
  Local Option in McLennan County, 1885 25

3 "The Steady Step and Majestic Swing of the Hosts of Reform":
  The 1887 Campaign for Statewide Prohibition 45

4 "The Blood of the Mighty Dead Has Stained Me!":
  Eggs and Honor in the 1887 Campaign 71

5 "Who Brought this New Idea into Texas, Anyhow?":
  Texans Reject Prohibition 89

Coda: From a Regional to a National Reform 103

Notes 121

Index 147

Acknowledgments

Like so many historical monographs, this project began, a very long time ago, as a graduate seminar paper that would not stay contained. A number of my teachers at Harvard offered criticism, advice, and encouragement, but particular gratitude is due Stephan Thernstrom, David Hall, and William R. Hutchison. Char Miller at Trinity University read and improved chapter drafts on several occasions. Bill Hutchison was also helpful in securing financial support and in providing a forum to first test my conclusions. His Harvard Colloquium in American Religious History has long been a place of nurture and sustenance for scholars and scholarship. Peter Koelling, Jeffrey Moran, and Thomas Clarkin have been generous with suggestions, counsel, and friendship.

Without librarians there would be few historians. I am indebted to the outstanding librarians at the Widener Library at Harvard, the Roberts Library at Southwestern Baptist Theological Seminary, the Coates Library at Trinity University, and the San Antonio Central Library. The staff at the Barker Center for American History at the University of Texas at Austin were knowledgeable and accommodating. The librarians and archivists at the Texas Collection at Baylor University, The Institute for Texan Cultures, The Texas State Library and Archives, and the Daughters of the Republic of Texas Library were always patient and helpful. The editors of the Southwest Historical Quarterly were not only kind enough to print my research on Frances Willard the first time around, they now have granted permission for that article to appear here, in revised form, as Chapter 1. David Holcomb, Carey Newman, and Diane Smith at Baylor University Press worked hard to make this little book better.

I am particularly indebted to my parents, James W. Ivy and Sue Eppes Ivy for their support, encouragement, and grandparenting skills. With grace and restraint they watched a son attain middle age in pursuit of a youth's dream. I am grateful for the goading of good friends, Peter and Demetra, Robert and Judy, Jeff and Susan, Keith and Sonya, and my brother Jeff. A long view on things of significance is the historian's conceit. My sons, Travis,

Zachary, and Samuel, are helping me to attain the genuine article. But my greatest debt is to my wife, Linda Ivy. Anyone who knows us knows this could not have been accomplished without her.

James D. Ivy
San Antonio, Texas
Thanksgiving 2002

Introduction

Southern Strategies

Eben L. Dohoney received a letter from Frances Willard in December 1899. We know this because he reported it in a book he published in 1903. In the letter, Willard praised Dohoney's latest book, wishing for it "the commendation of the world." She also recalled their work together for the cause of temperance in Texas when, as president of the Woman's Christian Temperance Union (WCTU), she had visited the state. Willard wrote that they had "labored under great difficulties; it was not a bed of roses," but reflected that "though the numbers were few, good seed was sown."[1]

It is worth noting that when Dohoney received the letter from Willard, she had been dead for nearly two years. The communication had been accomplished through the offices of a California medium. I mention this not to call into question the veracity of Dohoney's account, for, except perhaps for her favorable review of his book, there was little in the letter as he recorded it that is not consistent with what we know of these two people through more conventional sources. Nor do I mean to suggest that Dohoney's interest and confidence in Spiritualism diminishes his role as a nineteenth-century reformer. A number of American reformers of the era, including Frances Willard herself, were keenly interested in Spiritualism. A former Greenbacker, a lecturer on phrenology, and an advocate of women's rights, Dohoney was a prominent temperance advocate. He was responsible for the inclusion in the 1876 Texas constitution of a provision for local option elections. In 1884, he ran for governor on the Prohibition party ticket and served with Willard on the platform committee of the national Prohibition party. At her death, Willard was president of the WCTU and the most famous woman in America; when she earlier had visited Texas in support of prohibition she was already a nationally known reformer. The significance of Dohoney's letter from Willard is that it illustrates two things about his role in the Texas prohibition campaigns. First, as Willard reportedly noted, an arithmetic evaluation of their efforts would find that they fell short, despite their continued hopes for success. Second, Dohoney saw opportunity and value in working with Willard, a northern woman with a broad range of reform goals. Not all of Dohoney's Texas colleagues were as religiously or politically unorthodox as he, but most were willing to work with Willard and her organization, at least in the early days of their campaign for prohibition.[2]

For half a century, prohibition was the chameleon of American politics. Ubiquitous, it permutated and blended into the social landscape, absorbing and reflecting Americans' concerns about other issues. In the years between the end of Reconstruction and the U.S. Senate's rejection of the Treaty of Versailles, the nation struggled with urbanization, immigration, industrialization, economic turmoil, racism, and feminism. Somehow the question of the state's role in regulating the consumption of beverage alcohol became inextricably tied to each. Newspapers and politicians worried that immigrants drank too much, that cities bred saloons which bred other vices, that the production and consumption of alcohol was a drain on economic productivity, that African Americans should not be allowed to drink, or that women should not be allowed to tell men not to drink.

Historians likewise have provided a miscellany of interpretations to explain the perseverance of prohibition in the late nineteenth and early twentieth centuries. Richard Hofstadter believed it to be a reactionary anachronism of nineteenth-century reformers infected by the "rural-evangelical virus." Joseph Gusfield saw it as a struggle pitting "small-town America and commercial capitalism" against "a nationalized culture and an industrial economy of mass organizations." Others reversed the formula. K. Austin Kerr presented the Anti-Saloon League as an innovative and successful model for modern pressure groups; John J. Rumbarger saw the powerful hands, and pocketbooks, of industrial capitalists as the driving forces behind prohibition. In the history of feminism prohibition has been persuasively established as an early proving ground for nascent feminists and as an unfortunate detour on the way to social and political equality. In political history it has been both an irrelevant distraction and the best measure of voter participation and party loyalty. Prohibition has been interpreted as an assault on the urban poor and working class by middle-class zealots and as an attempt by beneficent middle-class reformers to improve the lot of exploited workers and their families.[3]

The various interpretations are wildly divergent, on occasion mutually exclusive. But a student of the reform could find them all persuasive.

Prohibition was a genuine issue concerning particular social ills, but it was also a prism through which reformers and their opponents could view the dramatic changes of modern life. It is no wonder that the historical interpretation of the reform has projected an equally broad spectrum.

Recently, historians have turned their attention to the political activities of southern women, particularly in the years between the end of Reconstruction and the First World War. Even without the vote, southern women were able to influence public policy, pressuring white male politicians to accept a larger role for state governments in relief and reform efforts. Breaching racial barriers, black and white women worked together on a number of causes, including prohibition. These efforts often ended in disappointment for black women as their white counterparts abandoned them in the early years of the twentieth century, but they provided an alternative to the clear lines of racial and gender politics that white male Southerners often practiced.[4]

One thing is clear: In the 1880s some Texans thought that other Texans were drinking too much. Ironically, Americans in that decade likely drank less alcohol per capita than do Americans today, but this is in some ways beside the point. Even the best statistics on consumption in the nineteenth century are rough estimates, given the ease with which beverage alcohol can be, and was, produced. Sales figures of taxed liquor do not tell the full story. Moreover, it was not just the practice of drinking, but the occasion and setting that offended many temperance advocates. The prohibition movement in the late nineteenth century was first and foremost a campaign to abolish the saloon, associated as it was with lawlessness and vice. In urban America the saloon also embodied for native-born Americans the advancing threat of immigrants. In the southern states in particular, the saloon, in the years before Jim Crow, was the setting for fraternization across racial lines, a situation that threatened to undermine the bulwark of social order, white supremacy.[5]

Another certainty in Texas in the decade after 1880 was change. In the previous two decades the state had been through Civil War, Reconstruction, and the reestablishment of Home Rule. The population of the state had doubled in just over ten years. A bare majority of all Texans had been born in the state, a majority of adults had not. Cities and towns were springing up along new rail lines; land was being newly cultivated, fenced, or grazed. Most Texans were on the move or recently settled, and for those who were not, the landscape around them was changing rapidly.[6]

The prohibition movement in Texas was in part a response to all of this change, uncertainty, and anxiety; but it was not simply a manifestation of a reactionary impulse. Prohibitionists were genuine reformers; they wanted to change the society around them. As reformers, they needed to accomplish two things. First, they had to demonstrate a need for their reform, that their vision of a new Texas was a beneficent one. Second, they had to persuade their fellow Texans that their reform was viable. To demonstrate the benefits of prohibition they employed strategies that temperance advocates had developed over decades of effort. They compiled statistics on the human and economic costs of alcohol, they told melodramatic stories of broken lives and homes, they warned of the evils of the saloon. To prove that their cause was a viable one they developed, gradually, a strategy that emphasized the continuity of prohibition with southern culture.

The term "southern strategy" is borrowed from the politics of the mid-twentieth century, when Republicans consciously appealed to southern white conservatives to try to break the domination of the Democratic Party in the South. Following Barry Goldwater's suggestion that they "go hunting where the ducks are," Republicans emphasized their party's allegiance to states' rights over federal intervention in desegregation. For twentieth-century Republicans the strategy worked. White conservatives abandoned the party of their fathers in a watershed realignment of American politics.[7]

Like all historical analogies, the application of the term "southern strategy" to events in Texas in the 1880s is not a perfect fit. Certainly, the campaign rhetoric and strategies that the prohibitionists developed over the course of the decade were intended to appeal to white southern males, and, it turns out, these were precisely the voters who endorsed the reform in the end. And, as twentieth-century politicians brandished coded language—"states' rights" or "law and order"—to appeal to regional prejudices, prohibitionists also were sensitive to the power of political invective. The difference was that the prohibitionists found themselves the objects of derision. They were characterized as "carpetbaggers" or "scalawags" for importing a northern reform. Particularly common, and damaging if left unanswered, were slurs that associated prohibitionists with antebellum northern reformers, "long-haired men and short-haired women" who had championed abolition, religious radicalism, or feminism. Rather than employ language to appeal to a regional bias, prohibitionists had to prove that they were not what their opponents said they were. Unfortunately for Dohoney and Willard, they too closely matched the type.

Prohibitionists did not begin the decade sensitive to these rhetorical aspersions. Dohoney played an important role in the early efforts; Willard's Texas tour was by every measure an unqualified, highly visible success. However, as the campaigns progressed and a core leadership developed in advance of the statewide battle, prohibitionists downplayed their connections to radical reformers, national organizations, and female leaders. They developed a southern strategy that characterized prohibition as a reform with southern roots in Texas soil.

Mrs. S. M. Baines of the Texas WCTU holds a photograph of Francis Willard. Unknown photographer; published in the *San Antonio Light*, November 8, 1933.

The UT Institute of Texas Cultures at San Antonio, No. 0119-1. Courtesy of The San Antonio Light Collection

Chapter 1

"The Lone Star State Surrenders to a Lone Woman"[1]

Frances Willard's 1882 Texas Tour

Texas was wet when Frances Willard left Texarkana en route to Marshall on February 3, 1882. The town of Denison recorded over three and a half inches of rain the previous month. More than eight inches had fallen on Galveston. With her companion and personal secretary Anna Gordon, Willard had been on the road for several weeks, stirring up support for the temperance cause, braving the early spring rains. Leaving Little Rock, Arkansas, they crossed into Texas over the swollen Sabine River on a Texas and Pacific railroad bridge that would be destroyed by flood waters a week later.[2]

Willard had served as president of the Woman's Christian Temperance Union (WCTU) since she defeated incumbent Annie Wittenmeyer at the 1879 convention by a large majority. Even before her election propelled her into the national spotlight as the leader of the largest women's organization in America, Willard was an important figure in reform circles. She had served as president of the North Western Female College at Evanston, had won a wide reputation as a speaker and as a member of the staff of evangelist Dwight L. Moody, and had held office as president of the Illinois WCTU and corresponding secretary for the national Union.[3]

The principal purpose of the tour was to organize local chapters of the WCTU in the southern states. The organization was formed in the wake of the "Woman's Crusade" that swept the Midwest and some eastern states in the winter of 1873–1874. Beginning in small Ohio towns, "praying bands" of women had publicly protested the presence of saloons in their communities, often managing to close the offending establishments and extracting pledges from the proprietors to abandon the trade. Hoping to sustain the movement, a group of reform-minded women met at Lake Chautauqua,

New York in August 1874, and called for the first convention of the WCTU to be held at Cleveland, Ohio that November. Under the leadership first of Annie Wittenmyer, then after 1879, of Frances Willard, the WCTU soon became the most visible temperance organization in the United States. Its members pledged to abstain entirely from beverage alcohol, and worked to combat the influence of the saloons in American life. Particularly under Willard's guidance, the organization expanded its agenda to include other reforms. At the convention at which Willard presided before beginning her southern tour, the WCTU adopted Willard's proposal for limited female suffrage, the "Home Protection" ballot.

The WCTU provided American women with an unprecedented opportunity for organization, cooperation, and public service. Women who had never been publicly active began to develop a network of communication and activism. The WCTU was not a female auxiliary of a male reform organization; in fact, men were excluded from active membership in the organization. After assuming the presidency, Willard worked tirelessly to expand the range and size of its membership. Her efforts, and those of other WCTU organizers, were rewarded as local unions formed and grew. However, in the southern states progress was slower.

For a variety of reasons, southern women proved much more difficult to enlist in the cause. The conservatism and paternalism of southern society closely circumscribed the public activities of women, and few southern women expressed any desire to challenge their role. In the northern states evangelical churches provided many women with their first experiences in social activism, most commonly in temperance work. In contrast, southern evangelicals generally eschewed social activism and its association with antebellum abolitionism. In addition, rural isolation and the disruption of western migration made it impossible for most women to participate in the wider associations of a national reform movement. Finally, southern women were themselves suspicious of an organization based in the north, associated with female suffrage, and dedicated to the participation of women in the public sphere. Still, Willard had made significant inroads. Her excursion into Texas came toward the end of her second tour of the southern states, a tour which had attracted both record crowds and national attention. For the first time in decades, southern women were meeting and working with their counterparts in the northern states. And her reception in Texas would demonstrate that there was a significant number of reform-minded women and men who were anxious to embrace Willard and her cause.[4]

Texas was booming when Willard arrived. The population of the state nearly doubled between 1870 and 1880, and the growth of the towns and cities was even more dramatic. Although barely a tenth of the people of the state lived in urban areas in 1880, the rate of population increase in town was almost twice that in the country.[5] Most of the newcomers were migrants from other southern states, although a significant number were from the lower Midwest. For the new and the older Texans, the years following Reconstruction were a period of disruption and change, bustle and promise. Things were not settled. The decision to build a spur line on a railway could transform the economy of an older village, or could leave it a ghost town. The Democratic Party was unsure of its grip on power, and reformers appeared to pose a real threat to the newly reconstituted Bourbons. African Americans, so recently freed from bondage and then disappointed by the failure of Reconstruction, had not yet been silenced by Jim Crow. Poor farmers had not yet slipped irredeemably into the peonage of the crop lien and shares. Roads were inadequate, governments were overwhelmed, and some people appeared to be making money by the bale. Intemperance, broadly speaking, seemed the order of the day.

If lawlessness was not pervasive it was a persistent problem in many communities, and the saloon stood as a visible sign of disruption, disorder, and vice. Willard was not the first to come to Texas to preach the temperance gospel. James Younge, lecturer and organizer for the United Friends of Temperance (UFT), had arrived over a decade before and had stayed. He organized hundreds of locals that worked through moral suasion, and occasionally through the legal coercion of local option, to combat drunkenness. The evangelical Protestant clergy, particularly the Methodists and the Baptists, had railed against the sin of drink from the pulpit and in print. Greenbackers, Alliance men, and labor agitators fought the saloon. Still Texans drank.

Willard's entrance into the state did not go unnoticed. She visited sixteen of the most populous communities, and at each spoke to record crowds. The press accounts of her meetings were numerous, thorough, and with only a few exceptions, flattering to the point of adulation. Her tour corresponded with, and vitalized, early efforts to impose statutory prohibition in Texas on both the local and state levels. Despite the divisive nature of the issue, she was received warmly by Texans who supported prohibition and by those who did not. When she left the state there were very few newspaper readers who were unaware of her visit and the extraordinary impression she had made.[6]

Nevertheless, within a few years, prohibitionists in Texas, even many of those who warmly greeted her in 1882, rarely mentioned Willard. Moreover, Willard's tour has virtually disappeared from the historical record, and where it is mentioned the details of her visit are often recorded incorrectly. The fact is that in the years following her visit to the state, Texas prohibitionists made a strategic decision to distance themselves from Frances Willard and her national organization. In 1882, however, Frances Willard took the state by storm, the herald of a movement that would be at the center of the state's politics for the next five decades.[7]

On Willard's brief foray into the state the previous year, she had met Eben Dohoney. Dohoney secured her a venue at Babcock's Opera House in Paris when none of the churches would condone a woman speaking from the pulpit. For the 1882 tour, Dohoney undertook to lay out the route of the campaign through the principal cities and towns of the state.[8]

At Marshall, the weather cleared briefly after three days of continuous rain, and despite the last-minute change in her schedule, Willard drew an audience beyond the capacity of the Cumberland Presbyterian Church. Listeners crowded, filling not only the pews but the aisles as well. Many stood in the churchyard, listening at the windows and open doors. A correspondent of a Galveston paper reported that "the lady spoke for one hour, and held the audience spell-bound by her delivery." When she and Anna Gordon left Marshall for Jefferson later that evening, they left behind a newly formed local WCTU with more than forty members pledged. After two appointments at Jefferson, Willard made a brief stop at Clarksville for one lecture, and then on to Paris, where she had visited the year before.[9]

It was at the invitation of the Paris union that Willard had added Texas to her itinerary, and she was embraced by the community upon her arrival. She renewed acquaintances, spoke with community leaders, visited the home of Eben Dohoney, lectured twice to a house "full and running over" despite the inclement weather, and recruited new members for the local union, already the strongest in the state. Lamar County was one of only four dry counties at the time of her visit, having enacted countywide prohibition by popular vote under the provisions of the state constitution, and the local WCTU was credited with getting out the vote on the issue. From Paris, Willard and Gordon took the Texas and Pacific west to Sherman. The rain had not let up and rivers and streams were overflowing their banks throughout the country. Because of the danger of washout, the train was running backward to protect the engineer and fireman.[10]

Not only did the rain make travel difficult, but it hampered communication. Willard had stayed in close contact with her mother in Evanston throughout her southern tour. Both she and Gordon wrote Mrs. Willard frequently, reporting on their successes, describing the people and the countryside, and keeping up with news from home. With the flooding of rail lines and bridges, Willard was cut off from a source of strength. She also worried about her mother's health. She dashed off a telegram before leaving Paris, with a brief but pointed message: "No letter from home Are all well Answer Sherman Texas."[11]

Sherman was one of two stops Willard made in Grayson County. It and its neighboring community, Denison, had a combined population of over ten thousand; in 1870 Sherman numbered fewer than fifteen hundred, Denison less than one thousand. Despite their recent establishment, the communities were situated in some of the most valuable farmland in the state, and Grayson was the most populous county in Texas. Most of the buildings in Sherman were newly constructed, but the town was already developing a solid, middle-class appearance. "The town is built in brick; there is a handsome courthouse and other public buildings; the architecture . . . is of a modern character," one observer wrote approvingly, "and the entire look of the town is business-like and metropolitan." Sherman was a trading center for surrounding communities and for interstate commerce, situated as it was at the intersection of the Houston and Texas Central, the transcontinental division of the Texas and Pacific railroads. However traffic was interrupted on a branch of the latter line fifty miles to the south by a washout on the east fork of the Trinity River the evening Willard arrived.[12]

The train pulled in at the Sherman station just after dark. Willard was scheduled to give two lectures at Sherman, but had already missed the first appointment the previous day on account of the railroad delays. To make her second meeting she rushed directly from the station to the Southern Methodist Church. When she arrived, an audience filling the pews and jamming the aisles greeted her. Mrs. J.W. Hearne, the president of the local union, opened the meeting. The crowd sang the hymn "Stand Up for Jesus," and Hearne introduced Willard, who proceeded with a reading from the second chapter of Joel. Willard was followed by the Rev. Dr. McLesky, who offered prayer and then presented Willard to the audience for her lecture. After she spoke, Mrs. Hearne returned to read the pledge of the WCTU, and a committee of men was appointed to obtain signatures from those in the audience willing to sign. A meeting for young people was scheduled for the next day at three o'clock at the Methodist Episcopal Church, and the Rev. Dr. Bourland, minister at that church, pronounced a benediction, closing the proceedings.[13]

After the Saturday afternoon meeting, Willard made the nine-mile trip north to Denison. Again, she was on familiar ground, having visited that town on her tour the previous year. The Denison papers printed updates of her schedule, and reported the preparations that were being made by the women of the local WCTU in expectation of Willard's arrival. In anticipation of an address on the subject, the meeting of the city council that week was marked by a lively debate concerning local option. Even the local saloon keeper took up the issue. A newspaper ad notified "the patrons of Yeidel" that free sandwiches would be served in his establishment following the lecture at the opera house. Yeidel added "no collection [would] be taken up to defray expenses," an obvious jab at the frequent practice of local unions to take up collections at the end of Willard's lectures.[14]

Pressing on to the south, the two women crossed the rolling central plains of the state, stopping at McKinney, Dallas, Fort Worth, Waco, and Georgetown. At each town record crowds enthusiastically received them and locally prominent citizens hosted them. Their efforts at organization continued apace. Despite the hardships, Anna Gordon could report with satisfaction that they were "traveling on through the mud of this immense state planting the WCTU here and there, and having tremendous meetings all along the line."[15]

The press reports of Willard's lectures and organization activities confirm Gordon's optimism. Typical was the report of the correspondent for the Sherman *Courier-Chronicle*, who after attending Willard's lecture in that city, hailed it as "perfect, unanswerable, and cover[ing] every part of the ground. . . . Miss Willard could do no more for the temperance cause here than all the committees, papers, and temperance tracts in Christendom."[16]

Willard planned two stops at Austin, the state capital. It was crucial to the success of her campaign that Willard be well received there. Her first meeting in the city was an affair of church and state. Joining her on the stage of Millett's opera house that Wednesday evening were the ministers from three Protestant denominations and the president of the local chapter of the WCTU. Also on stage, presiding at the meeting and introducing Willard, was Captain Thornton Hardie Bowman, who when he was not leading temperance meetings served as secretary of state in Governor Oran Roberts' administration. In a town accustomed to political pageantry and speeches, the decidedly anti-prohibitionist Austin *Statesman* reported that Willard "was listened to with the closest attention and was frequently applauded."[17]

Thursday morning, before leaving Austin for San Antonio, Willard wrote a letter to Mary S. Hathaway, the secretary of the Paris WCTU, reporting on her progress since she left that town two weeks earlier. "Within ten days we shall have fifteen local W.C.T. Unions in grand young Texas," she wrote, "and to-day your state has more auxiliaries than any other in the south except Maryland." She also had instructions for Hathaway. First, she suggested that the Paris union call a state meeting to coordinate the efforts of the various local chapters. To expedite this move, Willard enclosed a detailed outline for a state meeting with suggestions for "temperance literature, papers and general supplies" to have on hand when it convened. Second, she appointed Hathaway "state organizer" for the WCTU, with the responsibility for establishing new local unions and "strengthening those already planted." Hathaway was to report quarterly to Sallie Chapin in Charleston, South Carolina, who served as Superintendent of the South for the national organization. Although Willard herself was primarily responsible for the decentralized structure of the WCTU that granted more authority to women at the local level and allowed them to establish their own priorities for reform, she instructed Hathaway on the benefits of cooperation. "It would greatly encourage and unify our works if the different societies can be placed in practical and sympathetic relationships to each other," she wrote, "to the state of Texas, and to the National W.C.T.U." She also suggested cooperation with other temperance organizations, admonishing Hathaway "not [to] forget Brother George Baines and his 'Texas Prohibitionist' at McKinney." Finally, in a postscript, Willard suggested to Hathaway the means to facilitate the process of communication among local unions and their sympathizers. She wrote simply, "I am grateful for the kindness of the press." Hathaway forwarded the letter to the Paris *North Texan* for publication. She added a note, duly published in the paper, that after the plans for a statewide convention had been realized she too would take the field and tour the state "for God and home and native land."[18]

Willard had been cautioned by her supporters in north and central Texas to stay away from San Antonio, but she kept to her itinerary that had her in the River City between her two Austin stops. Certainly, the demographics of the city did not suggest that she would find audiences so amenable to her message as those in towns to the north and east. More than a quarter of the population of Bexar County was foreign born, and many of the natives were Tejanos and German-Texans who were unlikely to support Willard's cause. Even among the Anglo-Texans there appeared to be less support for any sort of organized reform. "Heretofore all efforts to organize a temperance society have failed on account of lack of enthusiasm on the part of the leading citizens," one editor lamented. "There are more saloons in that town than there are in Austin when the Legislature is in session."[19]

Despite the inauspicious conditions, Willard was received as enthusiastically in San Antonio as she had been elsewhere in the state. On the evening of February 23, a crowd packed Trinity Methodist Church an hour before the lecture was scheduled to begin. Joining Willard on the platform were several ministers, newspaper editors, and prominent citizens of the city, including George W. Brackenridge and Sam Maverick. Alderman William Heofling demonstrated the support of the German community with an address on the deleterious effects of beer drinking, and the Beethoven Glee Club provided music for the occasion. Staunchly opposed to prohibition, the principal newspapers of the city nevertheless battled to provide the most comprehensive and glowing account of the meeting. After criticizing previous temperance lecturers, whose "hackneyed and worn out phrases . . . have been thundered from the prohibition stump for years and years past," the correspondent for the *Daily Express* was overwhelmed. "Miss Willard has a clear, distinct, musical voice that charms all her hearers at once, and makes them interested in her subject and opens their stony hearts to conviction," he gushed. "She is always logical in her arguments, choice in her language, and has a wonderful fund of beautiful similes, apt quotations and beautiful illustrations that carry us along with her even though it be against our will." A reporter for the *Evening Light* was even more awestruck. The *Express* says Miss Willard the temperance lecturer "has a wonderful fund of beautiful smiles," he misquoted in his infatuation. "We'll take one." Another account described Willard and Gordon as "among the most highly cultured women of our country, and at the same time the most benevolent persons who ever visited our city."[20]

A cold rain fell on San Antonio the next day, but Willard and Gordon continued their appointments. In the afternoon, Willard met with a large group of women and organized a local union. At five o'clock, Anna Gordon addressed an audience of children and organized a "Band of Hope," the children's auxiliary to the union. That evening, the two were the guests of honor at a huge social gathering at the Methodist church, to which all of the town's citizens were invited. Despite the bitter weather, the church was packed with people hoping to meet the two famous women.[21]

On Saturday morning, the twenty-sixth of February, Willard and Gordon boarded a train for a return trip to Austin. For weeks the two had been jostling through the southern states, each day facing new crowds composed of enthusiastic well-wishers, the skeptical curious, and the occasional heckler. When Willard was not on stage addressing an audience, she was meeting with supporters, renewing acquaintances, smiling through endless introductions. There was little solitude even at the end of the day. To economize on her tours (and to avoid even a hint of impropriety) it was her practice to stay as a guest in private homes rather than in hotels. It was only en route from town to town, in the relative anonymity of a coach car, that

Willard could take the time to reflect on her situation. On the train Willard poured out her heart in a letter to her mother.

Despite her urgent pleas, Willard still had no news from her mother. Mail delivery from the north had been cut off entirely for several days, and she had received no answer to her latest telegram. Her concern for her mother's health was now compounded by a strong sense of isolation. "Never in my life—not even in Europe," she wrote, "have I felt so cut off from my own kindred." She complained of the "long days with constant meetings & people & goings on," and of the weather. "One single sheet of rain that fell a few days since brought down as much water than an entire average rainfall of any of the last eleven years." She also confided that it was her mother's example that gave her the strength to carry on in her mission. "You were always grandly equal to all of life's emergencies & have taught me some what of the same undaunted spirit." Renewed by her confession, she closed on a positive note: "Anna & I are marvelously well & successful in our mission of good will to the women of the south." Despite the difficulties they had encountered, Willard and Gordon had reason to believe that their efforts were being rewarded.[22]

Both Willard and Gordon had appointments that afternoon in Austin. Willard spoke to a female audience on "the duty of women in the crusade on intemperance." In addition to her duties as Willard's private secretary, travel agent, and confidant, Gordon usually took charge of meetings for children. In her lectures to children Gordon would illustrate the evil effects of strong drink by contrasting a saucer of alcohol and a saucer of water. At first glance, she pointed out, the two liquids appeared very similar. She struck a match and touched it to the saucer of alcohol. As the alcohol erupted in blue flame, she explained to her suddenly attentive audience that the same effect occurred in the brain of a dissolute drinker. A second match lighted and dipped in the water was instantly quenched. Gordon recruited substantial numbers of impressionable young people for a "Band of Hope" auxiliary with this simple and vivid demonstration.[23]

On Sunday afternoon, Willard was back in Austin, lecturing one last time at Millett's Opera House to an audience that packed the hall "from pit to dome." The Travis County Attorney called the meeting to order, and five ministers of the city joined Willard on the platform. The Musical Union of Austin provided the chorus. An invitation was also proffered to the newspapers to send representatives to join Willard on stage, and a number appeared both as reporters and as participants in the proceedings. Once more Willard managed extensive and favorable press coverage, despite the skeptical attitude most of the city's editors displayed toward the cause of prohibition.

From Austin, Willard and Gordon traveled east on the Central Texas Railway to Brenham, for a hastily arranged meeting at the Methodist church. After her lecture, she boarded the "night down-train" for Houston, where she stayed with supporters, then rose early on Tuesday the twenty-eighth to catch a train for Galveston.[24]

Galveston was the largest city in Texas in 1882 and one of the busiest ports in the South. The southern evangelical churches did not dominate the religious life of the community, as was the case in the towns of north and central Texas. Willard could not count on an enthusiastic welcome even among the city's reformers. And the weather was still threatening. More than three inches of rain had fallen on Galveston in the four days before Willard's arrival. Another three quarters of an inch fell the morning she arrived. But by two o'clock in the afternoon the clouds had broken up and the sun was bright in the sky.[25]

Willard spoke that evening at St. John's Methodist Church, home to one of the largest congregations in the state. Although a recent arrival to the state, the Rev. Mr. George W. Briggs was a leader among Texas Methodists; he drew the largest salary of any Methodist minister in the Texas conference, and would serve as editor of the *Texas Christian Advocate* for six years. At the end of the lecture Briggs offered two resolutions that were duly adopted by the unanimous assent of those present. The first was an expression of thanks for her address. The second resolution "commend[ed] her to the kindly sympathies and cordial hospitalities of our fellow-citizens of the South and . . . bid her a hearty God-speed in her noble mission."[26]

The last stop on Willard's tour of the state was Houston. The rain had finally stopped, and the Houston *Daily Post* reported that "the improved condition of the streets, the cloudless weather, balmy spring atmosphere, and the beauty of the moonlit night, very largely contributed to fill Pillot's Opera-house with a large and most respectable audience." The *Post* reporter appeared to know little of Willard's background. He was aware that she "was working in behalf of an organization she called the 'women's Christian Temperance Union'," but did not understand why she kept referring to Chicago, speculating that it was a city "against which . . . she seems to have a particular antipathy." Nevertheless, he was favorably impressed, calling her a "noble representative" of the temperance cause. On Thursday, March 2, the forty-sixth anniversary of Texas independence, Willard and Gordon organized one more union, then boarded an eastbound train for New Orleans. The *Texas Christian Advocate* bid her farewell, noting that "Miss Willard has certainly endeared herself to the people of the Lone Star State."[27]

Willard could leave the state pleased with the results of her visit. She left in her wake sixteen local unions, a state organizer, and plans for the establishment of a statewide organization. By 1885 there were sixty local unions, two "Young Ladies' Unions," and forty "Bands of Hope" in Texas. Two years later there were approximately a hundred unions. These local unions immediately began attracting attention by organizing social gatherings, reporting on their meetings and temperance work in local papers, and raising funds for reading rooms and libraries. Many of the women recruited by Willard in her southern tours would remain active in the leadership of reform movements for years to come.[28]

Equally as important as the boost Willard's visit gave to her own organization was the degree to which her tour catalyzed and brought together a range of temperance sympathizers. Willard was welcomed, encouraged, and supported by male reformers at each stop. In her brief visit to the state the previous year, Willard had difficulty finding places to speak. In the intervening year local unions and male prohibitionists worked to build a network of support. By the time Willard returned to the state, established politicians and religious leaders vied to share her podium.

Recently, historians have successfully documented the active role that women in the South played in post-Reconstruction politics. In most cases these efforts required looking beyond the narrow realm of electoral politics to uncover the activities of female reformers who could not vote but who could nevertheless work to redefine the political issues of the day. Women built alliances across lines of race and gender in support of prohibition and other progressive causes. In some states these alliances were shattered by the heightened racism that marked the era of Jim Crow, but the groundwork was laid for reformers who wanted southern state governments to address social issues beyond the construction of racial barriers. In Texas recent work has focused on the first decades of the twentieth century, when women, often within fairly conservative organizations, worked to enter the public sphere and broaden the scope of government activity.[29]

A visible result of Willard's tour was a dramatic increase in agitation for local option. Although the state constitution of 1876 provided for local option prohibition, efforts to outlaw saloons had been sporadic and usually unsuccessful. Willard's visit galvanized the temperance forces, and elections were called all across the state in the weeks during and following her tour. In some communities her visit coincided with the campaign, and she took an active role. In other places her lectures, and the press reports of them, sparked an effort to vote out liquor. The *Texas Tribune* of Paris reported that the local option election scheduled for Marshall was "of course the result of Miss Willard's address at that place." But while Willard was able to speak to the issue of prohibition without generating a great deal of hostility, the local campaigns brought to the surface deep divisions. Accusations of fanaticism and political opportunism were made on both sides. Newspaper editors entered the fray, or else tried to remain aloof and inoffensive with studied irresolution. The Dallas *Daily Advance* was a typical case. Its editors took a cautious approach to local option, suggesting that the issue be postponed until the fall elections. On the same day the paper came out foursquare against the sale of oleomargarine, demanding that the "poisonous article" be "banished by law from the markets." The newly formed WCTU locals were active and outspoken in the campaigns, often forgetting the virtues of Willard's generous tone. When Mrs. McPherson, a reporter for the Sherman *Democrat*, opposed local option, the Fort Worth *Democrat-Advance* suggested that the local WCTU "tackle" her. A Fort Worth WCTU member responded to the paper, asserting her belief that "the best thing to tackle any woman who advocates the whiskey traffic is a drunken husband." Agitation for the cause became so pervasive that one Fort Worth saloon keeper renamed his establishment in its honor. "While some people are worrying themselves about how to prevent men from drinking, others are inquiring where the finest wines, the purest liquors and the best cigars may be found and enjoyed," he noted. "Such men are always directed to the princely Local Option Saloon." Despite the unprecedented attention to the issue, most of the elections in the weeks immediately following Willard's visit returned large majorities for continued licensing of saloons. Willard had energized many who supported the temperance cause, and impressed a great number with her intelligence and conviction, but she had not immediately converted the state wholesale on the issue of statutory prohibition. Nevertheless, the agitation for local option continued, and within three years of her visit, scores of communities throughout the state voted on local option.[30]

The temperance movement in Texas had often skirted the blurred line between personal reform and social control. Since the provision for local option elections in the 1876 constitution, ad hoc organizations had emerged in a number of communities to petition for local elections. There also had been more sustained efforts. The Friends of Temperance, preceding the WCTU in Texas by twelve years, was a secret fraternal society pledged to personal abstinence. The primary tool of the organization was moral suasion, but its leadership had been instrumental in an unsuccessful effort to lobby the state legislature to submit a statewide prohibition amendment to Texas voters in 1881. A second attempt to get a prohibition amendment was made after a group of Protestant ministers met at Waxahachie in December 1881, and a prohibition convention was called for April 1882. Willard's tour coincided with these efforts, along with a wave of local and statewide prohibition campaigns throughout the southern states. Willard strongly endorsed these efforts toward statutory and constitutional prohibition. There was even talk of having Willard address the increasingly politicized Farmers' Alliance on Washington's Birthday, but that plan never materialized. It was difficult for either supporters or opponents to ignore the fact that Frances Willard was conducting a political campaign.[31]

In December 1881, at the beginning of her southern tour, Willard had forwarded to the *National Liberator*, a prominent reform periodical, a letter whose author she did not identify. It was a lengthy analysis of the state of reform politics in the southern states, particularly highlighting the success of William Mahone, the extraordinary leader of the Virginia Readjusters who had cooperated with that state's Republicans to turn out of office the Bourbon Democrats. This same feat could be accomplished in Texas, this anonymous writer continued, if the Greenbacker Wash Jones could be induced "to promise affiliation with the Republicans." The goal of this sort of fusion in Texas and other southern states was not to facilitate the reemergence of the Republican Party. Since the party of Lincoln had abandoned its reform roots, it would be superseded by the Prohibition Party. Willard did not explicitly endorse the arguments made in the letter, but she was impressed enough to make the document public.[32]

The printing of this letter apparently went unnoticed in the Texas press at the time. At Willard's first appearance in the state, even those few papers who regarded her critically made no mention of it. Nor was Willard implicated when, two days before her arrival in Dallas, handbills appeared in that city announcing a "grand Republican mass meeting at Fort Worth," to be addressed by, among others, Governor John St. John of Kansas, who had pioneered the adoption of state constitutional prohibition. The Galveston *Weekly News* was one of many papers that denounced the upcoming event, warning of a "politico-theological organization [that] will join with the prohibitionists in the next State campaign, in support of a prohibition ticket." The rally never materialized. Local Republican leaders denied any knowledge of it and dismissed it as a hoax, but Democrats were put on their guard.[33]

Then, in mid-April, after Willard had left the state and a few days before the scheduled prohibition convention, a number of articles appeared in several Texas papers accusing Willard of complicity in plotting to destroy the

Democratic party. One account had it that Willard was the chief conspirator in a "republican religio-prohibition alliance combination [that] has been secretly organized under the patronage and fostering care of the Woman's Christian Temperance Union." Another writer reminded readers that Willard was a member of the "Northern" Methodist church, and that her arrival preceded by only a few days the establishment of a "great morality party." The WCTU, "the legitimate offspring of the prohibition failures, and the lineal descendant of Miss Willard," was little more than a front for the Republican efforts to establish libraries in Texas towns to disseminate "temperance and Republican tracts." Editors warned that "Miss Willard . . . came down South, the hireling of the Republican party, not . . . to advance religion and morality but to use her best licks in endeavoring to destroy the Democratic party."[34]

Many prohibitionist leaders rallied to Willard's defense. At the convention meeting in Waco, Eben Dohoney was the first to rise in condemnation of the newspapers. He was followed by a number of others, and a committee was formed which drafted a resolution excoriating several editors and praising Willard and her work in hagiographic terms. The Rev. John Allen was appointed to draft a rebuttal to the charges. He asserted that "Miss Willard came to Texas upon the invitation of the Christian ladies, not as the hireling of anybody." Vague about her origins, he wrote that "Miss Willard came from Mississippi to Texas . . . with [the] assurance that a courteous reception and generous hospitality would be extended to her by the people of the state." Of the Paris WCTU that sponsored the tour, he wrote that "every officer in it is a Southern lady," and that most were Southern Methodists. His reply was printed as a letter to the editor in a number of papers, but it is likely that more readers saw the original accusations. Certainly Willard's critics had found a potent weapon to discredit interloping reformers. Allen's defensive regionalism only served to highlight the prohibitionists' acknowledgment of vulnerability on the point.[35]

For many of her critics, it was not only as a Yankee that Willard merited censure. As a woman, speaking from the pulpit, engaging in political discourse, working for social reform, she overstepped the bounds that circumscribed the role of women in nineteenth-century society. In the North her caution, her moderation, and her generosity towards adversaries blunted much of the criticism. However in the South, where gender roles were closely linked to the maintenance of the racial order, Willard's public activism posed an intolerable threat to her critics.

There were rumblings in some quarters that Willard was a suffragist, but Willard managed to sidestep this issue with a bit of calculated prevarication in the pages of the *Texas Christian Advocate*. More problematic was the simple fact that she was speaking publicly. From the first days of her tour of the state Willard had faced criticism for engaging in such "unwomanly" behavior. The editor of the Denison *Democrat*, while admitting that he did not attend Willard's lecture, was harsh in his denunciation. "On Saturday evening the people of Denison listened to the lecture of one of God's creatures who had stepped out of the sphere in which her Creator placed her and taken upon herself the duties belonging solely to a man," he wrote. "When Christ wanted apostles he chose men, not women; when Rome needed a general to command her armies, she sent to Cincinnati [*sic*] not to his wife . . . and we do not believe that the cause of temperance, religion or education will ever be benefitted by these female spouters of memorized compositions." As news of Willard's tour spread, more critics would raise questions about its propriety.[36]

Particularly troubling was the division that began to appear in the leadership of the Texas prohibitionists regarding Willard's role. Although most of the religious and secular newspapers sympathetic to the cause closely followed her progress in the state, there were noteworthy exceptions. The widely circulated *Texas Baptist*, a paper that was instrumental in organizing efforts for a statewide prohibition amendment and that reported weekly on local option elections, completely ignored Willard. Editor R.C. Buckner was not just an influential journalist. He was president of the Baptist General Association of Texas, proprietor of the Texas Baptist Publishing House, and General Superintendent of the Collection of Funds for the Buckner Baptist Orphan's Home, the Texas Baptists' premier social welfare program that bore his name. The associate editor of the paper was Benajah Harvey Carroll, a young Waco minister who was already perceived as a rising star among Texas Baptists and who would play a leading role in the prohibition campaigns for years to come.[37]

Willard's name never appeared in print in the *Texas Baptist*, but a week after she left the state the paper published a long piece entitled "Dethroning American Queens" that offered an extensive list of charges against women speakers. "Take a woman out of her sphere and you dethrone a queen; place her before the public as a politician or an advocate from the rostrum, even of social reform or religion, and you rob her of her God-given retiring modesty and weaken her influence over man," the editorial warned. The writer then went on to present the inevitable slippery slope of female visibility: preaching would lead to stump speaking which would lead to political involvement. Before long one would "hear the voices of men and maidens, of negro women and the cultivated wife and daughters of our own race, shouting . . . in our streets and at our country voting places." Only a decade before, "especially in our dear South-land, women but seldom appeared in the pulpit and on the platform; now . . . they travel the whole country over on lecturing tours, and make speeches in court-houses; and public halls." These women may be well meaning, but the inevitable result of this sort of behavior was social disorder, and the appearance of "female infidels," "female sleight-of-hand performers," "female gamblers," and "female horse-jockeys." For southern women, the public sphere was fraught with peril.[38]

Throughout the South, women had similar experiences. On the one hand, the WCTU provided a legitimate and generally respectable avenue for reform-minded women to have a public voice. Significantly, the organization was the vehicle for cooperation with male reformers, and occasionally bridged the racial divide to include African American women. On the other hand, the women of the WCTU, at least those who spoke publicly and tried to influence political debate, ran afoul of prickly southern males who tried to cultivate a paternalistic vision of southern womanhood. In parts of the South the coalitions held long enough to provide the groundwork for twentieth-century suffragists and prohibitionists, even if African Americans were abandoned in the process. In Texas, the events of 1882 seemed auspicious for women hoping to effect change in a turbulent society. The reaction of many of the men who ought have been their allies gave less reason for optimism.[39]

The impact on the political arena of Willard's visit brought into sharper focus issues that would be central to the prohibition campaigns in the state for decades. Despite the overwhelming success of her speaking tour, despite the visible results in local organization, prohibitionist leaders apparently decided that on balance an alliance with Frances Willard was more a liability than an asset. In the years immediately following Willard's tour, the core leadership of the prohibition movement in Texas outside the WCTU adopted a conservative strategy that excluded many potential supporters. They believed that if prohibition were to succeed it must be presented to the voters of Texas as a homegrown notion, uncorrupted by connection with northern reformers. Prohibition was pitched in such a way that it might appeal to Democrats anxious about the rise of competing political parties. A few prominent prohibitionists, such as Dohoney and James B. Cranfill, retained their loyalties to reform parties, but these were increasingly marginalized as a new generation of leaders came forward. These new men (and outside the WCTU they were inevitably men), in order to persuade local politicians and a state legislature dominated by Democrats to take up the issue, deemphasized the role played by political reformers and crusading women in stirring up support for the cause in the first place. Willard was vulnerable for two reasons. As a Northerner engaging in political agitation, she posed a threat to the southern Democracy; as a woman stumping for social reform, she threatened the southern patriarchy. The growth of the WCTU in the South heralded the possibility of a new direction for southern politics, a political culture less paternalistic, less racist, less regionally entrenched. White male prohibitionists in Texas would seek a more conservative route to reform.

Reverend Doctor B. H. Carroll, Sr.

Courtesy of The Texas Collection, Baylor University, Waco, Texas.

Chapter 2

"The Voice of the People is Voice of God"[1]

Local Option in McLennan County, 1885

The years following Willard's Texas tour witnessed an unprecedented surge in prohibition activity, at both the state and local levels. However, the WCTU did not provide the leadership for these efforts. Instead, white male political and religious leaders took center stage. This usurpation did not occur at once in a pitched battle for control of the movement. Rather, beginning in various local option efforts, white men reasserted their control of political issues, assuming (in every sense of the word) leadership on the podium and at the polls. As the movement developed, it changed in two ways. First, as women receded into the background, the public face of prohibition became the face of a white male. But the men who led the prohibition fight also recast the terms of the debate. Alcohol remained a threat to the family, the saloon an evil institution, prohibition a means to improve society, but these assertions were reformulated in a regional context. Rendered vulnerable by their association with northern political reformers and activist women, Texas prohibitionists began to develop a southern strategy in which their cause posed no threat to the white male's dominance of the social order.

Of course, in the Texas context, the social order was itself contested terrain. In the 1880s much of the state was frontier, much undergoing rapid development. Law enforcement was often lax, from lack of resources or lack of interest. However, stable communities were emerging, and, as in much of the South, dominated by a white, Protestant middle class. Particularly in the northeastern sections of the state, prohibition found support. Ellis and Limestone Counties were dry, and Anderson, Navarro, Smith, Tarrant, Hill, and Grayson Counties were debating or scheduling local option elections. However, the most closely watched local option vote in 1885 was in

McLennan County. Its county seat, Waco, was fast becoming the center of white, evangelical culture in Texas, and the headquarters of the state's prohibition movement. A victory there would be an important prize for the movement's leadership.

On the eve of Independence Day 1885, supporters of Waco University held a rally at the courthouse to raise money for the expansion of facilities at that flagship institution of the Baptist General Association of Texas. That the project received enthusiastic support from a broad range of the town's inhabitants was evidenced by the large crowd and the variety of speakers engaged. In addition to the prominent Baptist leaders, businessmen, and local politicians at the podium, the meeting featured a speech by U.S. Senator Richard Coke. A citizen of Waco since 1850, Coke had served as a captain in the Confederate Army and as an associate justice on the Texas Supreme Court. His election as governor in 1873 marked the end of Reconstruction in Texas, and in 1877 the legislature sent him to the United States Senate. At six feet, three inches and two hundred forty pounds, with a flowing white beard and a booming voice, Coke commanded attention at any public event.[2]

Coke was ebullient in his praise of the university, pointing to its remarkable accomplishments in training a generation of Texans despite the limitations of the current accommodations. "If any man doubts that Waco University is a power in Texas, let him tread over Texas and mingle in business and political circles as [I have] done, and his doubts will pass away," he asserted, and he particularly extolled the efforts of President and Rev. Dr. Rufus Burleson and his faculty. Nevertheless, while the civil and religious leadership of the community were in perfect harmony regarding the value of an expanded educational institution, they would soon be divided in an acrimonious struggle over the sale of alcoholic beverages in Waco.[3]

An early catalyst to the local option campaign that summer was a revival preached in the city by the Methodist evangelist Sam Jones. Jones preached two sermons a day for a week and as many as four thousand attended some of the evening meetings. The newspapers of the state closely followed the revival; the Waco *Examiner* printed the text of several of his sermons and followed up with articles and editorials. A popular and pugnacious orator, Jones drew criticism for his rough treatment of local minsters, but in the main his sermons, and particularly his attacks on saloons and drunkenness, received enthusiastic reviews. Wacoans concerned about the easy availability of liquor had reason to hope that public sentiment was with them.[4]

Later that month, on the morning of July 21, approximately 150 delegates convened at the Odd Fellows' Hall on South Third Street in Waco for the State Grand Council of the United Friends of Temperance (UFT). Representing nearly 100 local councils and claiming a membership of over 34,000, they gathered to celebrate the expansion and strength of their organization and to formulate plans to further the cause of temperance in the state. Most in attendance were young men, but also among them were several veterans of temperance reform. The delegates voted to give President Burleson, a founding member and former officer but no longer there in an official capacity, a seat on the floor and the opportunity to make a speech. Dr. James B. Cranfill, a prohibition editor and generally regarded as the likely next Prohibition Party candidate for lieutenant governor, represented the membership at Gatesville. But preeminent was Dr. James Younge, the organization's Grand Lecturer, who first had visited Texas in 1854 on a temperance lecture tour and subsequently settled in the state after the civil war, continuing his efforts to enlist workers in the cause.[5]

The UFT was a respectable and conservative organization; it did not pose a threat to the political or social order. Established at Chattanooga, Tennessee in 1872, the fraternity originated in a schism in the International Order of Good Templars. The founders of the UFT objected to the inclusionist racial policy of the Good Templars, and to the older organization's close ties to the Prohibition Party. Although a number of the leaders in the Texas UFT maintained ties to the partisan Prohibitionists, most members were loyal Democrats. The organization continued without question the policy of excluding African Americans, but retained the Good Templars' practice of including women. Laura Towers of Thornton and Cora Kimbrough of Cotton Gin were delegates, and a number of women attended as guests of the Council. However, the UFT did not endorse female suffrage. There was little to indicate that the Grand Council would be much more than the occasion for moral exhortation and celebration.[6]

The delegates had considerable cause for celebration. Even if their membership claim is difficult to verify, they could demonstrate the organization's strength and viability in the aggregate receipts for the previous year in excess of $2,500, with a $388 surplus after expenses. Eight counties in the state had voted in local option elections to outlaw the sale of beverage alcohol, and eight more were dry in all precincts but the county seat. The numerous speeches dealt primarily with the success of local option in delegates' home communities, and the hopes that other counties and towns would soon follow. Between sessions the delegates retired to an anteroom, and raised to the cause beer glasses full of ice-water provided in barrels by County Sheriff Harris.[7]

The central issue facing the delegates was what to do next. Like many of the fraternal temperance organizations of the nineteenth century (and excepting the parent organization, the Good Templars), the UFT did not enunciate a particular political agenda; instead it emphasized moral suasion and the support of fellow teetotalers to discourage drinking. But many delegates had connections to other organizations and other agendas. James Moore, in addition to delivering the welcoming address to visiting delegates on the opening day of the Grand Council, was also the chairman of the ninth congressional district for an *ad hoc* Prohibition Convention which had met the previous May in Dallas. In that capacity he was charged with furthering the cause of statewide prohibition in his district. On the day the UFT Council convened, Moore published in the Waco papers a call for a convention of the citizens of McLennan County, to be held on August 1, to consider the nomination of Prohibition candidates for public office and the "transaction of any other business that may be deemed proper to secure the abolition of the whiskey traffic, either by local option or constitutional prohibition." Any delegate in town who picked up a local paper would have seen Moore's call featured prominently alongside the news of the Grand Council's opening session.[8]

On the last day of the meeting, Dr. Cranfill, in his capacity as the chairman of the Committee on the State of the Order, presented what was supposed to be an assessment of the organization's development over the previous year. But after briefly rejoicing in the growth in membership, he offered a course of action. He formulated his plan as a prescription for advancement of the UFT. "That the state of the order may be improved," he suggested that "in as many counties as is possible a vote be taken on prohibition in the coming September." As he warmed to his subject, it became clear that he was issuing a call to arms. "Pulverize the rum power must be written on every banner and the burden of every song," he declared. "God has said it; civilization has said it; common humanity has said it, and the saloon must go."[9]

In accordance with James Moore's call, a convention met the week following the UFT Grand Council at the McLennan County courthouse to decide how best to further the temperance cause. It was an inauspicious beginning for a campaign that would soon dominate the public life of the county. Fewer than thirty participants had appeared by the appointed hour of eleven in the morning, so the meeting was adjourned for three hours so that the leadership might round up more supporters. Even so the convention was not called to order until 2:30 in the afternoon, with about forty in attendance. The first order of business, after the election of officers, was to debate the advisability of seeking a local option election for countywide prohibition. Speakers expressed concern regarding the likelihood of victory, and the ability to mobilize support for the cause in the short time available once an election had been called by the county commissioners. Colonel J.M. Anderson expressed the view that "it would be folly to enter the contest without thorough organization," and that "if the friends of prohibition are not ready to make war against whiskey, then the meeting had as well adjourn, and the friends of the movement go home." But the discussion that followed allayed his concerns, and he offered the motion that the commissioner's court be petitioned at its next meeting to order an election. Those present endorsed it unanimously. In an effort to get an early start in the campaign, the convention appointed chairmen for each precinct, with instructions to begin immediately to organize voters and to enlist speakers.[10]

Getting the measure on the ballot would require the cooperation of local political leaders. A predominantly Democratic legislature had consistently rebuffed prohibitionist efforts to submit statewide prohibition to a vote, and it was unclear whether local party leaders would support even a countywide effort. Captain William Reed declared his willingness to leave the party "if it did not go for prohibition," and his remarks were received politely, but nervously, by his colleagues. Prohibitionists did not want to be seen as political spoilers, threatening the dominance of the southern Democracy. One of the reasons that support for the WCTU had evaporated so quickly three years earlier was Frances Willard's association with third-party Prohibitionists, or worse, with Republicans. White Texans who might otherwise sympathize with the temperance cause would turn away from its political manifestation should it prove to be a vehicle for overturning the post-Reconstruction political order. Colonel Anderson rose to speak, assuring the house that political schism would never need to be on the table. The Democratic Party, he asserted, "would never be found defending the whisky men."[11]

The issue of loyalty to the party of the fathers set aside for the moment, Anderson then brought up the subject of race. He averred that the cause of prohibition could be furthered with the "active cooperation of the colored voter," whom he viewed as "ripe for the prohibition movement." This remark prompted the Rev. Taylor to rise. He was an African American veteran of the effort who had traveled extensively throughout the state; he most recently had canvassed Denton County prior to a prohibitionist victory in a countywide election there. Rev. Taylor agreed that the "better class of Negroes" were ready to support prohibition, and that, moreover, they were willing to "break down the republican and democratic parties in order to clear the field for the fight against the whisky demon." He suggested that African Americans be appointed assistant chairmen in each precinct, to help to get out the black vote and to "touch the pride of the race." The convention voted to accept Taylor's proposal, and a committee was designated to facilitate the appointments.[12]

The political power of African Americans was a factor with which both sides in the prohibition debate would have to contend. Since the end of Reconstruction intimidation and fraud had curbed the influence of black voters. Nevertheless, systematic efforts to disfranchise African Americans had not begun in most southern states, and black Texans in particular would retain access to the ballot into the twentieth century. If there was a danger that white voters might be put off by a political movement that openly courted the black vote, it was offset by the possibility that African Americans might provide the margin of victory. Prohibitionists would have to find a strategic middle ground to accommodate both white and black sympathizers. The Rev. Taylor's appeal to the convention to distinguish the "better class" of African Americans provided them an opening.[13]

With the organization and basic strategy decided, the convention voted to raise one thousand dollars, then adjourned until August 12, by which time the county commissioners should have considered the petition for a vote. Meanwhile, opponents of prohibition began to take steps to counter the effort of the temperance reformers. Before the prohibitionists' petition was presented to the commissioners' court, Waco attorney John Dyer filed his own petition, requesting a local option election for the city of Waco. When the commissioners met in session the following week, they faced an awkward dilemma. The legislation providing for local option elections required county commissioners' courts to call timely elections following petitions for local option by citizens of precincts, towns, cities, or counties. If the petition were found to be valid, they could not refuse it. Moreover, the law required that the election be held before the next session of the commissioner's court. The commissioners were constitutionally obliged to grant both petitions: one for a local option election in the City of Waco, the other for a local option election for all of McLennan County. But the statutory provision for holding local option elections also mandated that in the event an effort to outlaw alcohol failed, a local option election could not be repeated in a jurisdiction within a period of one year. Since it was expected that opposition to prohibition would be stronger within the city limits of Waco than in the rural precincts, Dyer's petition, if acted upon first, would have the effect of giving city voters the opportunity to forestall countywide prohibition for at least a year.[14]

Armed with a quickly obtained opinion from the state Attorney General's office, the commissioners were able to finesse the issue. They voted unanimously to grant the second petition first, setting the date of a county-wide vote for August 31. They then voted to consider the first petition on September 2, and adjourned with the parliamentary fiction that the September meeting would be a continuation of the July session. Thus they were able to circumvent the legislative prohibition against postponing action on the petition until a future session of the court. The prohibitionists were handed a procedural victory, and the anti-prohibitionists quickly filed suit to reverse the actions of the McLennan commissioners. There was scant case law for the state courts to rely on in deciding whether the commissioners had acted properly. However, events would preclude a definitive ruling on the issue when the vote was tallied in the county-wide election. The principal result of the affair was to focus even more attention throughout the state on the fight in McLennan County.[15]

The local chapter of the WCTU had languished in the three years since its organization by Frances Willard on her tour through the state. The local option campaign revived it. The women of the Union directed a "temperance concert" performed by the Sunday school pupils of the Trinity Methodist Church, organized a Young Ladies' auxiliary "to educate their young gentlemen friends up to a realization of the fact that there is some higher sphere of enjoyment than whisky drinking," and applied such pressure to the editor of the Waco *Examiner* to provide them with space for a weekly column that he felt obliged to respond to in print explaining why he couldn't afford to do so. And while their activities received regular coverage in the pages of the *Examiner* (despite the editor's opposition to their cause), and deferential tendance from the prohibitionists, they did not play a pubic role in the local option campaign. With the exception of one meeting organized by the WCTU, none of the numerous rallies held in the weeks before the vote featured female speakers. Instead, prohibitionists relied on prominent local men and visiting male celebrities to get out the vote.[16]

One local figure who quickly achieved prominence in the campaign was the Rev. Dr. Benajah H. Carroll. Born in Mississippi, Carroll had moved as a child with his family, first to Arkansas, and then in 1858, to Texas. Like so many raised in the nineteenth-century South, he was exposed at an early age to both religion and strong drink. Every evening Carroll's father led the family in prayer; every morning he served them whisky. Although he had opposed secession, Carroll served in the Confederate Army and was seriously wounded at the Battle of Mansfield. In 1870 he responded to a call from the congregation of the First Baptist Church at Waco, and in 1873 joined

Dr. Burleson's faculty at Waco University, training aspirants to the ministry. That same year he demonstrated his devotion to temperance by pressing his congregation to adopt a strongly worded abstinence pledge.[17]

Carroll's first appearance on the podium in the campaign was on August 12, at a public rally scheduled to follow the action of the commissioners' court setting the date of the local option election. Probably as a result of the publicity surrounding the commissioners' action, over six hundred people turned out for the meeting, including a number of women. African Americans composed approximately one-sixth of the crowd, including a contingent from neighboring Bosqueville bearing a banner that proclaimed "Prohibition Now and Forever." Carroll was one of three speakers who addressed the crowd; and because of his office, he was featured as a speaker on "the moral point" of the issue.

Characteristically, Carroll did not confine himself to moral questions. He opened with a political defense of prohibition, arguing that it was consistent with both Democratic and Republican principles and should therefore not be made a partisan issue. He also responded to economic arguments put forth by anti-prohibitionists who had contended that should prohibition carry in the county, "grass [would be] growing in the streets, bats and owls would inhabit [the] public buildings." Acknowledging the importance of the economics of the issue, he challenged the conclusions of those alarmists. "If Waco cannot be supported by her great grain crops, her great corn and cotton crops and immense wool receipts, she certainly cannot be supported by her saloons," he argued. Nevertheless, he asserted that there were some things more important that economics. His declaration would have resonated with his southern audience: "Better let grass grow on the streets than have it cover dishonored graves." Finally, he urged prohibitionists to organize and prepare for the campaign ahead.[18]

That they were determined to do. In the evening session of the meeting, organizers were appointed in each of the thirty-one precincts in the county. Their mandate was to organize prohibition clubs, to be sure that speakers were scheduled in their precinct in the days leading up to the election, and to get out the vote on the critical day. In addition, thirteen African Americans were appointed to mobilize the black prohibition vote.

The next morning handbills appeared all over Waco announcing an anti-prohibition rally that evening. Originally scheduled for the courthouse, the meeting was moved to the town plaza to accommodate a larger crowd later in the day, then rescheduled for the courthouse when rain threatened. The district court room quickly filled as local citizens turned out to hear opponents of prohibition attack the measure. On the bill were Judges G.B. Gerald and George Clark, and General Sul Ross, already widely viewed as the frontrunner in the 1886 gubernatorial race. However, the highlight of the evening was expected to be the speech by Senator Richard Coke.

Senator Coke did not disappoint his audience. He began by reminding his audience that he had been a resident of Waco for thirty-five years, and questioned the need of prohibition in a community that had so successfully combated public vice in that time. He also expressed the concern that prohibition would handicap Waco in its economic growth. He challenged the assumption that prohibition would be effective in curtailing the use of alcohol, asserting instead that it would simply restrict the community's ability to regulate it. But he spent most of his time outlining the anti-prohibitionists principal objection to the reform, that it "is a direct assault upon the personal liberty of every man to be subjected to its operation."[19]

Coke's articulation of the "personal liberty" objection to prohibition was not the first time prohibition was attacked as an intolerable threat to individual liberties. But as he framed the argument it had a particularly southern subtext. For many of the white male Southerners who made up the majority of his listeners, Coke's admonition that "no man should willingly part with one jot or tittle of his personal liberty" would recall the same argument made in defense of the Confederacy. For African Americans, the notion that they should be vigilant in retaining rights so recently won would be at least as compelling.

But Coke's disquisition on personal liberty was not simply an exercise in political theory. Rather than refer to the legacy of the American Revolution, he sought to frame his argument in the context of a masculine culture of honor. "The personal liberty of a man should be like the virtue of a woman," he urged, "whole and perfect, beautiful in its symmetry, its harmony and entirety." Further evidence could be found in the larger political agenda of the prohibitionists, and the danger it posed to gender roles in southern society: "They hope, when our people are warmed up on prohibition, that they will also swallow female suffrage." Prohibitionists threatened to take from men more than a drink. Men who allowed encroachments on their liberties risked losing not just their freedom, but their manhood as well.

Coke elaborated further his objections to prohibition with an attack on the role of clergy in the movement. Referring both to Dr. Carroll's speech the previous evening, and the statement of the Rev. Mr. Jordan that black voters would "break down both political parties if necessary to carry prohibition," he deplored the involvement of religious leaders in a political movement. Noting that it was a development "happily rare in the south," he warned that, if not stopped, such involvement of the clergy would "[bode] no good to either church or state, religion or society." As an example, he recalled the abolitionism of the northern churches: "To more than any other one cause, we are indebted for the bloodshed, destructiveness, and woe of our great civil war, to the crusade of the northern churches against the political institutions of the south." The implications of the parallel would not be lost on many in his audience.[20]

Two other speakers followed Senator Coke at the podium, but their speeches received much less attention either from the press or from the prohibitionists in their responses. General Sul Ross, who had been scheduled to give the last speech of the evening, rose only to decline the honor, citing the heat in the hall and the lateness of the hour. He assured those present that he stood ready at any time to answer the call to speak against prohibition. But it was clear that for the time there was little to add. Coke had effectively thrown down the gauntlet in his challenge to the reformers.

With less than three weeks remaining and the local fight receiving increasing attention from the state press, both sides quickly mobilized. The anti-prohibitionists established a formal network of precinct workers and stump speakers to match the prohibitionist strategy. Leaders on both sides continued to issue manifestos in handbills and through the press. Within a few days of the initial organizational efforts, the Galveston *Daily News* reported that in Waco "prohibition and anti prohibition rallies are as numerous as bales of cotton of the new crop." The Waco *Examiner* declared that "McLennan will be the best canvassed county in America, by next Monday." Advertisers took advantage of the interest in the issue with announcements like the "challenge to prohibitionists and anti-prohibitionists," issued by R.P. Sturgis' dry goods store to try to find lower prices on boots, shoes, and hats. While prohibitionists were more successful in blanketing the county with speakers, the antis in particular were able to attract prominent politicians to deliver their message. In addition to Senator Coke and General Ross (who did finally address a rally in opposition to the reform), opponents of prohibition enlisted the assistance of Congressman Roger Q. Mills.[21]

Many politicians were hesitant to take a clear stand on the issue of prohibition, and particularly on the merits of local option as a means to that end. The notion that citizens acting locally could make policy for their own communities was seen as a particularly Democratic principle, and many state leaders continued to express that view, whatever their position on the merits of prohibition. In advance of the Waco vote, Lt. Governor Barnett Gibbs took the position that while statewide prohibition would be an infringement of individual liberty, a local community had every right to outlaw saloons. Congressman John Reagan favored criminalizing the sale of alcohol to minors and regulating the sale of adulterated beverages, but expressed the hope that prohibition would not become a political issue in Texas.[22]

Reagan was to be sorely disappointed. The "personal liberty" objection to prohibition was presented by the antis as the only position consistent with party philosophy. Congressman Mills entered the debate through an interview with the Galveston *News*, and elaborated on this view with language designed to appeal to southern males. Contrasting local option and statewide prohibition, he told his interviewer that "when a man's liberty is taken from him by his neighbors in his precinct he has fewer masters." But he saw no fundamental difference in the two policies, or their impact on the individual citizen. "His condition is unaltered," he concluded. "He is a slave to that extent." The proper course for partisan Democrats was to oppose prohibition as an invidious and intolerable threat to their freedom. "Before this invasion rides into triumph it will find itself confronted on every hill and vale in the land by the united hosts of democracy, and it will be buried so deep that the trump of the arch-angel will never awaken it from its long repose," Mills declared.[23]

Increasingly, the McLennan County campaign became tied up in a debate over the significance of prohibition in statewide politics. It also featured in an occasion of southern pageantry. In early August a number of politicians, including four expected to enter the race for governor in 1886, addressed a reunion of Confederate veterans at Fort Worth. General Ross, Congressman Reagan, Lt. Governor Gibbs, and State Comptroller William Swain each took their turn at the podium. According to a correspondent for the Galveston *News*, as the old soldiers listened to each of the speakers, "the cause they fought for was painted in glowing colors . . . and the victory won by the enemy twenty years ago was shown to be the very best thing that could have happened." And while the speech were fairly devoid of political content, off the podium most of the speakers admitted that "there is only one issue before them now, and how to avoid taking issue on that is what puzzles most of them." Of the four candidate Ross and Gibbs had taken a stand on prohibition. The others were clearly struggling to find a position.[24]

For partisan Democrats there were two distinct issues to consider: first, the position elaborated by Coke and Mills that prohibition was undemocratic in principle; and second, the fear that as a political concern prohibition threatened to divide and weaken the Democratic Party in Texas.

On the first point prohibitionists began to respond in earnest. Letters appeared in papers around the state from Democrats protesting the notion that they could not remain consistently true to the party and support prohibition. In particular, many were incensed that local option could be construed as party heresy when it involved the exercise of popular sovereignty at the local level. A writer from Mastersville, in southern McLennan County claimed that "the vote at this place will be about three to one in favor of prohibition." "When you remember that Blaine and Logan got not one single vote at this place at the last election," he continued, "the claim that prohibition is undemocratic does not seem very consistent, and won't go down with the people here." Prohibition editors vied to establish the purest southern Democratic credentials. After reprinting some of Congressman Mills objections to prohibition, the Rev. George W. Briggs, editor of the Methodist *Texas Christian Advocate*, observed that "born and reared in the South, and voting with the Democratic party ever since our majority, we claim the privilege of saying that we have heard that figure before." The editor of the Bonham *News* scoffed that the antis "might just as well say a man who favors Masonry cannot be a Democrat."[25]

The assertion that the prohibition movement posed a threat to the hegemony of the Democratic Party was a more troubling issue for the reformers. The difficulty was exacerbated to a significant degree by the frankness on the part of some to declare that they were quite ready to abandon the party if it became an obstacle to the movement. Not only had the local prohibitionists at their first meeting to organize the campaign discussed the possibility of a break with the Democratic Party, but many of their prominent allies had conspicuously suspect partisan credentials. The UFT Grand Council had featured a few party Prohibitionists, and when they left town others had arrived as speakers. State Senator William Homan made appearances in the county defending the political orthodoxy of local option, until Democratic editors began to point out that he had been elected as a Greenbacker, and that more ominously, he had been a supporter of the Republican state administration during Reconstruction. "When Homan was president of the Milam loyal league," the Waco *Examiner* asked, "was he rated a good democrat then?" His work for the cause and his political background were widely reported, and although prohibitionists at first rushed to his defense, they quickly began to downplay his role in the campaign and redoubled their efforts to demonstrate that "one and the same principle underlies local option and true Democracy."[26]

The suggestion that prohibition was a threat to the power of the Democratic party was particularly ominous for many white Texans. While there were certainly significant political issues contested in the closing decades of the nineteenth century in Texas and in the other states of the former Confederacy, the Democratic party maintained its hegemony in large part because of its legacy as the party that had turned back Reconstruction.

Texas Democrats were generally able to fend off challenges from Republicans and political dissenters like the Greenbackers of the 1870s by raising the specter of "carpetbag" rule. And while attacks on the political power of African Americans had not yet reached the pitch they would at the close of the century, most white Texans believed that their privileged position in society was best entrusted to Democratic leadership. Anti-prohibitionists exploited the racial fears of white partisans by implying that African Americans who supported prohibition were doing so in the hopes of "break[ing] down the democratic party." Neither side wanted to alienate the black voter, who still had enough political power to influence the outcome of the contest, but the prohibitionists faced a particularly difficult dilemma. If their adversaries could characterize them as the dupes of African Americans intent on challenging the Democratic establishment, they would lose support among whites who might otherwise be sympathetic to their cause. Nevertheless, they needed the support of as many black voters as they could recruit in what was sure to be a closely contested fight. Their solution was to segregate as much as possible the organization of the campaign, to acknowledge that the black vote would be divided, and to aver that "the better class of colored people" would support prohibition as a means of uplifting their race and combating vice and crime.[27]

But as the campaign progressed, prohibitionists increasingly found themselves on the defensive. In speeches and in editorials the antis continued to press their case that prohibition jeopardized the stability of the political order. Democrats had regained control of the state just eleven years earlier and white southern men were nervous about a new threat to their power. The Waco *Examiner* reminded readers of the Republican "efforts to repress the manhood of Texas and fix republican policy as the permanent rule in the state." The prohibition campaign was a thinly disguised effort on the part of Republicans to try again. The *Examiner* urged a martial response: "Let the men of McLennan . . . go to the front for democracy, for their manhood and for their liberty." By framing the issue in the context of politics, gender, and freedom (in patent contradistinction to slavery in the southern milieu) the opponents of prohibition had diverted attention from the merits of local option as a reform measure. Opposition was now an affair of honor.[28]

If the prohibitionists were to salvage their campaign they would need a champion with incontestible southern credentials. On August 16 the Rev. Dr. B.H. Carroll made it clear that he saw himself in that role. The local paper announced that Dr. Carroll would preach "a special sermon on prohibition" at the First Baptist Church that evening, specifically intended as a response to Senator Coke's address three days earlier. The two were suitable adversaries. Although Coke was Carroll's senior and a more illustrious figure statewide, Carroll had risen quickly to local prominence and was acknowledged to be the senator's equal on the stump. Moreover, the two were well matched physically, each big and tall and sporting flowing beards; they were credible patriarchs in a struggle over the future of their community.

Carroll addressed a crowd that filled "every pew and aisle" of the largest church in the city. His sermon began as an exposition on a passage from the nineteenth chapter of Acts, in which disciples of the apostle Paul are mobbed in Ephesus after an accusation by angry silversmiths who fear that the Christian message threatens their livelihood in crafting images of their goddess. When one of the disciples tries to speak to the crowd, he is shouted down. Carroll clearly had in mind the economic defense of the saloons and the reception that prohibitionist speakers often received before unruly crowds.[20]

Carroll opened his sermon with a reference to his own case. "It has been alleged that I have gone outside of a minister's true position to discuss politics," he began. He also pointed out that he had been accused of promoting the disruption of the Democratic Party, of endangering the commercial growth of Waco, and of making a "direct attack upon the personal liberty of every man in the county." These were serious charges, and he offered to address them each.[30]

On the issue of the Democratic orthodoxy of local option, he reviewed the legislative history of the local option statute. He reminded his listeners that General Ross had been a member of the constitutional convention that mandated the law, and that Richard Coke as governor had signed the bill establishing the procedure for local option elections. He attacked the economic argument as narrow and flawed, arguing that the financial cost of the liquor traffic was a much greater burden than any revenues derived from the sale of alcohol. The personal liberty issue, which the anti-prohibitionists had been emphasizing in their campaign, Carroll approached with legalistic caution. The local option law did not prohibit the consumption of alcohol, only its manufacture and sale. Citing an opinion of the federal Supreme Court, he pointed out that "no one can claim a license to retail spirits as a matter of right."[31]

Carroll devoted some time to a defense of the regional authenticity of prohibition. He countered the anti assertion that prohibition "is like the abolition of slavery from New England, and does not suit the South" by pointing out that the prohibition movement in the northern states was preceded by a Democratic measure to outlaw alcohol in the Indian Territory. More to the point, he cited the success of the movement in Georgia, Arkansas, and in several Texas counties as evidence that prohibition was a genuinely southern reform.

On his own role in the campaign, Carroll was defensive, even evasive. He was appointed to a committee to put before the people the reasons for supporting prohibition; he would do so without resorting to insult or demagoguery, and urged all involved to "rely upon argument, truth and moral suasion in conducting the canvass." He expressed his fear that the attacks on his activities indicated that the opposition would not be so restrained. From them would "come the croaking: Blue light, blue light, Mayflower, Mayflower, crank, crank, fanatic, fanatic . . . clergy, clergy, clergy." He made it clear that such attacks would not dissuade him from leading the prohibition effort. Nevertheless, his prickly self-defense highlighted the fact that his adversaries wielded a powerful weapon. The cause of prohibition could be handily discredited if it were linked to northern reform and reformers.[32]

Carroll's sermon was reprinted in full in the Galveston *Daily News*, the *Texas Baptist Herald*, in the local press, and as a pamphlet to be used in the campaign. It was the subject of editorials and letters in the press throughout the state, and was freely plagiarized and rebutted by speakers on the stump in McLennan County and other communities where prohibition was gaining a foothold or elections were scheduled. The sermon revived the flagging hopes of McLennan County prohibitionists and boosted Carroll to preeminence in the movement.[33]

The campaign continued to heat up as speakers on both sides of the issue blanketed the county. It was generally acknowledged that within the limits of Waco the vote would favor the anti-prohibitionists, so the rural vote was courted assiduously, particularly by the temperance forces. The antis did not overlook the country precincts, but focused their attention on the towns and devoted considerable resources to a final effort to get out the vote in Waco. The final rally in opposition to the local option effort was scheduled for Saturday, August 29, two days before the vote. Scheduled to appear were Congressman Mills, Senator Coke, and a number of other dignitaries.

The day before the meeting four barbecue pits, nearly a hundred feet each in length, were dug in a field adjacent to Padgitt's Park on the outskirts of town. The pits were filled with wood and ignited in the afternoon, and beginning at ten in the evening the meat was spitted and set to cook over the coals. A half mile of tables was constructed, about one third of the segregated seating reserved for African Americans. Major Wiley Jones, chairman of the committee on barbecue, oversaw the slaughter of fifteen cattle, twenty hogs, and seventy sheep. The committee also supplied three thousand pounds of bread and a variety of pickles and sauces.[34]

The crowd began gathering in downtown Waco early on Saturday morning and were entertained first by the firemen and then by the Oriental Cornet Band. Over three thousand proceeded from the plaza to the park, where they were greeted by a banner stretched across the gate which proclaimed "Eternal Vigilance is the Price of Liberty." By 11:30, when Congressman Mills rose to speak, the crowd had grown to between five and six thousand. Still recovering from a fever, Mills spoke only for an hour, but the Waco *Examiner* praised his address as "one of the greatest ever delivered by any man since Texas has been a state." The audience then turned its attention to the tables, and was allowed two hours to consume the feast. Afterward, Senator Coke took his turn at the podium.[35]

After brief and general remarks on the importance of the issue, Coke turned to clerical involvement in the campaign. "It is said by some ministers that the reason they discuss [prohibition] is because it is a non-political question," he observed. "Ah, my fellow citizens, whenever your preachers go into politics scourge them back." The crowd cheered, and he continued: "The worst signs of the times that I can perceive is to be found in the delivery of stump speeches from God's pulpit." Referring specifically to Dr. Carroll's sermon on prohibition, he declared it a political speech, "delivered from the pulpit of the church on a Sabbath evening under circumstances which preclude any reply or interruption." Coke spoke for two hours, devoting much of his time to responses to Carroll's sermon and further criticism of the minister's participation in a political struggle. He was followed by Judge George Clark; then the meeting was proclaimed a success, and the crowd sent home. As one local pundit observed, "A barbecue catches the patriots as nothing else will or can."[36]

Because the election fell on a Monday, the prohibitionists had the last word on the issue prior to the balloting. On Sunday, August 30, temperance sermons were preached throughout the county. Dr. Carroll spoke in the evening to a crowd of 1,200 packed into the First Baptist Church. But by midday Monday, even leading prohibitionists were quietly expressing the view that they would be defeated. The rural precincts were expected to vote dry, but not by a margin great enough to outnumber the opposition in Waco.[37]

Over five thousand voters turned out in the county, and the results were an even greater disappointment for the prohibitionists than expected. Soon after the polls closed it was reported that prohibition would be defeated by more than a thousand votes. The opponents of the measure took to the streets of Waco in force, bands played, and Senator Coke was serenaded at his home. Bonfires flared, and at one location an effigy resembling Dr. Carroll was set up to be burned, but rescued from the flames at the last moment. With the release of the preliminary count the next morning it was clear that prohibition had been defeated in McLennan County by a margin of more than two-to-one. Even the country vote went against local option; in only two rural precincts did the prohibitionists prevail. Within the limits of Waco fewer than one quarter of the vote went to the prohibitionists.[38]

Anti-prohibitionists and editors sympathetic to them were quick to view the vote in McLennan as a vindication of the opposition's position and as a death knell for the prohibitionist cause. The Galveston *Daily News* predicted that the defeat of the reform would "encourage its opponents in other counties of the State at present preparing to vote on the question," particularly since prohibitionists had made the fight in McLennan County "the center of the contest." The Waco *Examiner* reported that most citizens were relieved that the bitterness of the past few weeks had passed, and urged goodwill on all sides. In a series of editorials the paper predicted that the prohibitionists would recognize that they could not achieve their aims through the ballot box, and would return to the tried-and-true methods of moral suasion. The rancorous struggle had demonstrated once more that when clergy (and to the extent that they had been involved, women) participated in a political campaign "there is always greater bitterness and a more offensive degree of personalism than in a simple race when these potent influences are not particularly interested." Nor were their efforts effective: "The clergy of McLennan can lead the people to heaven almost without effort, but really they cannot lead them to the ballot box." They were likely now to heed the advice to stick to their calling.[39]

But the prohibitionists appeared undaunted. One Waco voter wrote the Galveston News to report that "the staunch Democratic voters of McLennan county are to-day Prohibitionists by an immense majority," an insupportable claim that was reprinted enthusiastically by the prohibitionist press. The *Texas Observer* blamed the defeat on "plenty of money and the negro vote." The *Texas Christian Advocate* reported that 190 foreigners obtained discounted naturalization papers just in time to vote against the measure, and that the antis "surrounded the polls with paid strikers" to discourage the temperance vote. There were yet more than twenty counties that were scheduled to vote on local option in the coming weeks, and "every county should fall into line, and if defeated, begin the struggle again and again." The prohibitionists did not appear to view theirs as a lost cause.[40]

A coda to the McLennan County local option fight demonstrated the determination and bitterness of the prohibition reformers. It also illustrates the increasing focus on offended masculinity in the rhetoric. The Rev. Dr. Carroll took to his podium once more to answer Senator Richard Coke. Carroll did not address the broader issues of prohibition, nor did he spend much time exhorting his hearers to carry on the fight in Waco. Instead he focused on Coke's attack on his participation in the campaign, and particularly Coke's call that the voters of McLennan "scourge back" the clergy who were involved in politics. He once again preached from the book of Acts, taking for his text a verse from chapter 22: "Is it lawful for you to scourge a man that is a Roman, and uncondemned?" Coke had been criticized for what was perceived even by some supporters as intemperate language. "I know not what import he attaches to the word 'scourge'," Carroll declared, "[but] I know how the people understood him." Carroll's sermon made explicit the link already in the minds of many who had heard Coke's remarks. Scourging was a punishment reserved for slaves in the antebellum period, not an acceptable treatment for any freeborn white Southerner. Coke's remarks were an attack on Carroll's honor.[41]

Carroll's sermon was reprinted widely, but it was George Briggs, editor of the Methodist *Texas Christian Advocate*, who took up the issue with a vengeance. "If there is a Christian minister in the State of Texas the free blood in whose veins does not leap at this insult, he deserves to be unfrocked," Briggs declared. "If there is a free citizen in the State who does not resent such outrageous intolerance, he does not deserve his liberty." In language recalling Chief Justice Taney's opinion in *Dred Scot*, he accused Coke of taking the position that "preachers of the gospel . . . have no rights as citizens that anybody is bound in conscience to respect." And if the implication was still unclear, Briggs wondered, "will not somebody do Senator Coke the kindness to inform him that the days of slavery are now over?" Coke had challenged the manhood of every minister in the state. Briggs expected that "Senator Coke's next proposition will be to put the preachers in bonnets and frocks." When the editor of the Galveston *Daily News* suggested that he was overreacting, Briggs accused the *News* of advocating the disfranchisement of the clergy. It was clear that at least a few of the prohibitionists had not accepted the antis' counsel to accept defeat quietly.[42]

Nevertheless, throughout the state, defeat was what the prohibitionists were facing. In local option elections they were losing badly, even in counties where they believed they stood a good chance of success. With the defeat in McLennan County the tide had turned. Within a few weeks local option was defeated in Navarro, Anderson, Leon, Milam, Hill, Grayson, Camp, Falls, Collin, Van Zandt, Madison, Smith, and Red River Counties, and in scores of local elections in precincts and towns. At Hempstead, just nine days after the defeat in McLennan County, prohibitionists lost in the city by a vote of 426 to 21. A torchlight procession and a brass band escorted a coffin reportedly containing the remains of prohibition to the public square where a grave had been dug with a whisky barrel placed as the headstone and a beer barrel at the foot. On the whisky barrel was inscribed "Sacred to the memory of Prohibition." But the report of its untimely demise was premature. Within two years prohibition would become the most important issue in Texas politics.[43]

The next campaign would be led by many of the same prohibitionists who had fought unsuccessfully for the reform in McLennan County. Learning from their experience in the local option fight, they began to organized earlier for a statewide effort. They also modified their strategy in the wake of defeat. In 1885 they had avoided association with female reformers, but drew criticism for the involvement of male clergy. In 1885 they responded by defending vigorously the right of clerics to be involved in the campaign. They did not reverse this position entirely, since clergy, in particular Baptists, would continue to play key roles. Nevertheless, in 1887, there would be a conscious effort to downplay their contributions. Before Texans went to the polls in August 1887 to vote on statewide prohibition, the reformers would craft their campaign to appeal to the sensibilities of southern white males. The McLennan County defeat insured the deployment of a southern strategy that would push to the margins "short-haired women and long-haired men," and would not threaten the dominance of the Democratic Party.

Chapter 3

"The Steady Step and Majestic Swing of the Hosts of Reform"[1]

The 1887 Campaign for Statewide Prohibition

There is little evidence to suggest that the supporters of prohibition were inclined to abandon the cause in the wake of the defeat in McLennan County. Reports of local option elections, temperance meetings, and appeals to local courts appeared in daily and weekly papers across the state with increasing frequency throughout the following year. Concurrent with this increased activity, pressure mounted on the state legislature to approve a constitutional amendment providing for statewide prohibition. In 1887 these lobbying efforts bore fruit with the state legislature voting overwhelmingly to submit to the voters of Texas a constitutional amendment banning the manufacture and sale of intoxicating liquors.[2]

The balloting was scheduled for August 4 of that year in a special election. There were six other amendments at issue, but no candidates for office would be on the ballot. In this way office holders (and seekers) could avoid, if they wished, association with the reformers or the anti-prohibitionists. Moreover it was hoped that the Democratic Party would not become mired in a struggle over the partisan orthodoxy of prohibition. The previous year in convention the state party had declared itself supportive of the principle of local option, but delegates did not take a corporate stand on their hopes for the results of local option elections.[3]

The prohibitionists knew that they faced an uphill battle to gain sufficient support for the measure to pass in August. Their experience in the defeat of local option in McLennan County taught them the importance of organizing early and broadly. They lined up prominent supporters and worked sympathetic newspaper editors for publicity and favorable reviews. They also fixed their political strategy. The role of women in the statewide campaign would be closely circumscribed. Issues of religious activism and race would be carefully managed. Support for the cause must be untainted by association with Northerners or northern ideas. These particulars would serve a broader effort to portray the leaders of the movement and the reform itself as genuinely southern and particularly Texan. It would be a reform that in no way would undermine the authority of white males.

Of course Texas was not the only venue for statewide prohibition reform. Temperance advocates had been waging campaigns for decades in a number of states to outlaw beverage alcohol with mixed success. Portland Mayor Neal Dow drafted the legislation that became the Maine Law of 1851, the model for a series of statewide prohibitory laws that were enacted in thirteen states and territories within a few years. However this antebellum wave of reform was limited primarily to the northeastern and midwestern states, and was short-lived. Delaware was the southernmost state to enact statewide prohibition before the Civil War. After briefly enduring the zealous enforcement of the prohibitionists, state after state abandoned the experiment. The dissolution of the Whig Party and the sectional crisis of the late 1850s further disrupted the movement. It was not until women took the lead in the 1870s that a revival of temperance sentiment reignited efforts to enact statewide prohibition. First in Kansas and across the west, by the 1880s several states throughout the nation were the settings of vigorous campaigns to outlaw liquor. In 1887, the year statewide prohibition was on the ballot in Texas, voters in Michigan, Tennessee, Oregon, and West Virginia also cast votes on the issue in their states.[4]

Texas prohibitionists supported the adoption of a constitutional amendment for several reasons, not the least of which was the prospect of eliminating the saloon in a single effort. The drafters of the 1876 constitution had ordained a system of local option elections as an improvement on the practice of special legislation for communities through the legislature, but local option clearly had its drawbacks. Town voters frequently frustrated the efforts of prohibitionists in rural precincts who failed to achieve countywide bans. Even when entire counties voted dry, liquor from adjacent wet counties could still be purchased and consumed. Local option victories also could be short-lived. An election victory one year could be reversed by a contrary vote the next, or invalidated by a state judge because of suspected voting irregularities. Constitutional prohibition had better prospects for longevity. A statewide ban by constitutional amendment could be voided only by a future amendment, a situation that one critic pointed out would mean that a handful of state senators could keep state prohibition from ever being reversed. Prohibitionists also felt that a significant benefit of a statewide campaign, not associated with campaigns for elective office, would be to take the issue out of the hands of unsympathetic or corrupt politicians. Recalling the influence of prominent politicians in the local option election battles in McLennan County and across the state, prohibitionists hoped that by distancing the issue from partisan politics, individuals might be more likely to vote their consciences rather than to follow the lead of famous politicians.[5]

Opponents of prohibition did not necessarily oppose the submission of the amendment. Gov. Sul Ross, who before his election to that office had spoken in opposition to prohibition in local option campaigns, urged in his opening message to the nineteenth legislature that they pass the amendment, giving the voters of the state the opportunity to declare once and for all their position on such an important subject. The vote for submission in the House on January 30 was 80 to 21, and in the Senate on February 25 was 22 to 8. There is some correlation between a legislator's opposition to submission and his constituents' eventual rejection of the amendment, but it is also clear that a number of lawmakers voted to submit the amendment and subsequently opposed its adoption. It is quite possible that many voted to submit the amendment in the hopes that they could put behind them an issue that had been a source of dissent and political uncertainty in home districts, whatever their personal views on the matter. The WCTU's *Union Signal* even suggested that some legislators were motivated by opposition to the measure, fearing that "if deferred two years and temperance sentiment advances at the rate it has done for the past two years, it will be sure to pass."[6]

The prohibitionists moved quickly to organize a campaign. A convention was called for March 15 at Waco, a town still regarded as a crucible of prohibition sentiment despite the setback of the 1885 local option campaign. Delegates began arriving on the fourteenth, and by ten o'clock the next morning more than three hundred delegates assembled to hear the Rev. Dr. B.H. Carroll, now serving as the chairman of the State Prohibition Executive Committee, welcome them to the Opera House for what one reporter described as the "largest State convention of the kind ever assembled in Texas." The majority of the delegates were white males, with African Americans composing approximately one quarter of the convention. Carroll introduced Dr. F.T. Mitchell, chaplain of the state House of Representatives, who asked for divine assistance in combating "the greatest enemy to society and the soul of men ever created by the machinations of the wicked one." Carroll then returned to the podium to state the purpose of the convention. He emphasized the secular, nonpartisan nature of the campaign. "We come here, not as preachers, not as religionists, not as Democrats, not as

Republicans," he insisted, "but as Prohibitionists, as citizens of Texas, without regard to race or previous predilections on any known question."[7]

The convention organizers hoped to broaden the appeal of prohibition by putting forward a number of prominent Texans who would not be accused of clerical activism or political radicalism. Following Carroll's suggestion that "the preachers will take a back seat and our offices be filled by men of standing and ability who are members of the secular professions," the delegates selected the aging Judge D.M. Prendergast as permanent chairman. While Carroll continued to function as the leader of the movement as the Chairman of the Executive Committee, none of the other principal offices were held by clerics. The commitment of the convention to appeal to as broad a range of voters as possible was highlighted when the Rev. D. Mathie of Seguin urged the convention to support the publication of a German-language prohibition newspaper. Even the color line could be crossed to reach out for support. Abraham Grant, an African American delegate from Austin, was selected as parliamentarian and as a member of the State Executive Committee. When he was subsequently referred to as a "colored brother" by one of the speakers, he rose to object, stating that he was not attending as a "colored brother," but as a prohibitionist. He continued, predicting that if the white voters of Texas would "do their duty," the black voters would likewise support the cause. He was applauded by the convention and the *Texas Christian Advocate* reported that "his speech was certainly a creditable one, doing honor to his race and giving prohibition a boost." But despite the efforts at a broad appeal, male prohibitionists at the convention avoided association with their female counterparts. There were no women among those chosen for positions of authority. The only female who was reported to have spoken publicly was Carrie Cox, a delegate from the Woman's Christian Temperance Union of Granbury. She did not address the convention in session, but was on the bill as part of one evening's entertainment; described as "an accomplished elocutionist," she "recited 'No Licence to Pave the Dark Pathway to Hell.'" The female prohibitionists took the role of incidental entertainment.[8]

After a lively exhortation by Dr. James B. Cranfill on financing the campaign, the delegates pledged a generous $15,000 for the cause, and began the work of appointing committees, drawing up organizational plans, and recruiting speakers. Dr. Carroll's State Executive Committee retained the authority for planning and financing the campaign. The members of the committee included dozens of prominent citizens from all across the state, but the day-to-day affairs of the campaign were to be handled by the ten local members at the Waco headquarters. A Committee on Address, also chaired by Dr. Carroll, issued a declaration "to the Prohibitionists of Texas," reprinted in a number of papers, outlining the work of the convention and the steps for local organization. The convention was adjourned by the singing of the doxology and a benediction pronounced by temperance pioneer Dr. James Younge. In less than three weeks following the passage of the proposed amendment by the legislature the prohibitionists had put together a campaign organization, raised a sizeable war chest, recruited a number of speakers to stump the state for the cause, and had reached thousands of voters in the press coverage of their activities. They had less than twenty weeks to prepare for the vote, but they were optimistic that these early efforts would improve their chances for success on August 4.[9]

Despite their low profile at the Prohibition Convention, women did not disappear entirely. They continued to work diligently for the cause in the months leading up to the August vote. Members of the Texas WCTU had begun campaigning even before the legislature voted on the prohibition amendment. State President Jenny Bland Beauchamp wrote to the *Union Signal* in January praising the efforts of a number of Texas women who were out in the field lecturing. With pride she reported that it was unlikely that "any southern state can show more of her own women at work in a public capacity" than Texas. The Union was a significant force in lobbying the legislature on the amendment, and also saw early successes in the drafting of a scientific temperance bill and in getting the age of consent raised from twelve to sixteen. Other temperance reformers, men included, appealed to the WCTU for assistance in organizing clubs and establishing reading rooms to further the cause. One supporter, John Belcher of Gainesville, surveyed the site of a new town on the Gainesville, Henrietta, and Western Railroad eight miles west of Nocono, and named it Willard, in honor of Frances Willard. The statewide WCTU sponsored visiting lecturers, including Emma Pow Smith of California, Annie M. Palmer of Iowa, and Sallie Chapin of South Carolina. And while it did not receive the press coverage that the Prohibition Convention had, the organization's state convention at Waco (at Dr. Carroll's church) in May was well attended, and Beauchamp and Corresponding Secretary Annie Horner were confident that the Union would play an active role in the campaign.[10]

Despite these efforts, male prohibitionists continued to resist a public role for female reformers, one member complaining that many sympathetic ministers could not bring themselves to announce from the pulpit forthcoming WCTU meetings. Those who would "are half afraid, and make the bare announcement with subdued voices, without comment." State Superintendent of Reconnaissance Fannie Rees Pugh reported that the "greatest drawback" facing the Texas Union was the association of the Union with the cause of female suffrage, despite the fact that only a tiny minority of the state's membership wanted to vote. Pugh counted herself among the radical minority. "If they will not let us make laws," she fumed, "I wish they would let us make the officers of the law."[11]

On occasion, prompted by attacks from anti-prohibitionist press or speakers, male prohibitionists rallied to the defense of their female counterparts. Interestingly, the men appeared to feel the sting of criticism themselves, rather than on behalf of the female targets. "We hear no more of 'short-haired' women from the Antis," the editor of the *Texas Baptist and Herald* scolded. "The honor of our Southern manhood was shocked by this unchivalrous slur upon our countrywomen." Judge Robert West emphasized the same theme in responding to criticism of women's role in the campaign: "O, young man, where is your boasted Southern chivalry? Stoop to hit a lady, will you?" Unlike most of his colleagues, West endorsed the activities of the women in the campaign. "There has nothing come up yet, from a bloody revolution to a school . . . election, that the ladies have not taken an interest in," he argued. "They are interested in what men are interested in, and go to battle for their friends, and every true gentleman admires them for it, whether they be on his side or not." However West's views were not held generally. More often male prohibitionists were as likely as their opponents to insist that women play a limited role in the campaign. The Paris *News* emphasized the distinction between the propriety of women endeavoring to influence men who would vote and any desire on the part of women to cast ballots themselves. The editor of the *Texas Baptist and Herald* observed with obvious satisfaction that "now that the W.C.T.U. of Texas has ignored female suffrage as a side issue, it is claimed that the pending amendment has gained many friends." The Dallas *Daily Herald* went even farther. Readers were assured that an event sponsored by the local WCTU was not a suffrage meeting, but was "purely a woman's temperance organization," in no way connected with the campaign for the amendment. The timing of the meeting was mere coincidence. The prohibitionist leadership was determined to marginalize women reformers rather than risk dismissal as a "crusade of preachers and petticoats."[12]

But even as they shed the petticoats, the prohibitionists kept the cassocks. Despite Carroll's cautionary opening remarks and the selection of officers at the Waco convention, clerics played a central role in the 1887 campaign. While the membership of the State Executive Committee included a number of judges, lawyers, and physicians, prominent ministers from around the state secured appointments and lent their names to the cause. At the local level, where the effort to get out the vote would be critical, clergymen were conspicuous leaders. And the great majority of traveling speakers were evangelical ministers who could stump for the cause during the week and return to their pulpits on Sunday.[13]

Particularly in rural communities and small towns, where the vast majority of Texas voters lived, it was the clergy who took it upon themselves to prepare the state for the August vote. W.T. Compere was a farmer and a part-time preacher in Cloverdale and Armer, two communities without organized Baptist churches. He wrote to the *Texas Baptist and Herald* to report that he had organized a prohibition club at Cloverdale, and that at his next appointment there he would preach on "the Bible on temperance and prohibition." The same paper reported two weeks later on the activities of Dr. A.S. Worrell, who served as minister to three Baptist churches in Lamar County: "He has been working hard in the interest of Prohibition, and expects to do a good deal more." The Rev. A.J. Holt, who was responsible for raising money to support Baptist missionaries in the state, feared that the prohibitionist preachers were campaigning too well. So much money was being collected for waging the campaign and supporting the prohibitionist speakers that churches were hard-pressed to fund any other missionary work.[14]

Historians have often found it useful to downplay the differences between the Protestant denominations in the South, referring instead to "southern evangelicals" as a cultural entity in contradistinction to Catholics or to northern Protestants or to more secular Southerners. But the leaders and members of southern congregations in the nineteenth century would likely not have subscribed to this ecumenical analytical shorthand. "Hardshell" Primitive Baptists and Missionary Baptists fought bitterly over theology, worship, and church polity. Methodists ridiculed Baptist doctrine and practice, and Baptists responded in kind; both Methodists and Baptists staged day-long public debates with Church of Christ "Campbellites," each side using scripture to demonstrate that the other was leading innocent souls down the road to everlasting perdition. Nevertheless, in the prohibition campaign there was an uncharacteristic spirit of cooperation of a sort not common since the white southern churches had enlisted together in the Confederacy's cause. Editor S.A. Hayden of the *Texas Baptist and Herald*, reported in detail on the prohibition work of his Methodist allies and editor Briggs of the Methodist *Texas Christian Advocate* defended B.H. Carroll when the Baptist prohibition leader was attacked for his role in the campaign. A number of prohibition rallies featured ministers from several denominations. Early in the campaign, when the WCTU's efforts were more frequently recognized, the Dallas Union sponsored an event at the First Baptist Church in which local Methodist and Presbyterian ministers participated. In March ministers from local Baptist, Methodist, and Church of Christ churches presided over a temperance meeting at the Workingman's Hall in the same city. And at Austin an Episcopal cleric joined a Methodist at the podium of a temperance "cake and ice cream festival." The secular papers also followed the activities of the campaigning preachers, printing the speakers' schedules in advance and offering extended reviews of their speeches. City papers covered Georgian Atticus Haygood's tour in detail and published a number of his speeches in full. Even the anti-prohibition press gave favorable reviews to the preachers. The Galveston *Daily News* reported that when the Rev. D.F.C. Timmins of the Shearn Memorial Church in Houston addressed a "Gospel Temperance Meeting" in that city the crowd was well behaved and the speaker was effective and well received. The correspondent concluded that "like nearly all the ministers of the state he is a pronounced and active prohibitionist," but did not object to his role in the campaign.[15]

The prominence in the campaign of clergy, despite the best efforts of prohibitionist leaders, drew criticism from many anti-prohibitionists. The tradition of clerical detachment from civic affairs was strong in the southern states, even if not always scrupulously followed. Opposition to slavery on the part of many southern evangelicals, more evident very early in the nineteenth century than in the late antebellum years, had provoked swift censure from secular authorities. The rise of abolitionism in the North and the support the movement received from a few prominent northern clerics further hardened Southerner's distrust of politically active preachers. Before the adoption of the 1876 constitution, the notion that it might be dangerous to afford clerics full citizenship rights was political orthodoxy. The prohibition campaigns revived the sentiment. Former Lt. Gov. Barnett Gibbs, a leading anti-prohibitionist, positioned himself as a moderate on the issue, declaring that he believed that preachers should share with others the right to participate in politics. "No man, no matter what his vocation is, should lose his identity as an American citizen," he declared. He simply objected to ministers preaching prohibition from the pulpit, exhorting congregations that "all Christians should vote as they pray." Gibbs opined also that preachers had overstated the evils of drink, suggesting that "there were more people in the insane asylum from religious enthusiasm than from whisky." Gibbs' criticism quickly drew responses from a number of prohibitionists who accused him of attacking both Christianity and the rights of citizens.[16]

The Baptist Benajah Harvey Carroll remained the most visible of ministers involved in the campaign. Newspapers throughout the state reported extensively the Reverend Doctor's actions, and regularly printed the text of his speeches. On Monday, May 2, he gave a speech at the Opera House in Dallas that drew an enormous crowd, including correspondents from several newspapers. Among the papers that reprinted the speech was the Dallas *Daily Herald*, which dedicated over two and a half pages of an eight-page edition to the text. The *Herald* also offered reprints of the speech to "prohibition clubs and newspapers for supplements" for six dollars per thousand. Carroll's speech had the widest circulation of any campaign document on either side of the fight, and in it he set forth in great detail the position of the prohibitionists.[17]

The published report of Carroll's speech was not the work of a newspaper stenographer. It included charts and tables to which he referred in making his case against the liquor traffic. Evidently he had a hand in the preparation of the printed version and presumably with the preparation of the reprint that circulated as a campaign pamphlet. Aware of its potential circulation and experienced in previous campaigns, Carroll would have known that his speech would be scrutinized closely both by potential voters and by his opponents in the amendment campaign. The speech was a long one, filled with extended quotations and references to statistical data on the social cost of alcohol consumption and the success of prohibition in other states, but the thesis was simple. Carroll asserted, with considerable documentation, that the social order was diminished by the saloon and by drunkenness, and that a prohibition amendment would be effective in eliminating the former and reducing the latter. He devoted several paragraphs to an indictment of the Liquor Dealers' Association of America and warned of their corrupting influence in politics. And he spent a great deal of his time reassuring voters that Texas prohibitionists had no political aspirations other than the passage of the amendment. The prohibition amendment was not a partisan issue or a religious issue, but a singular matter of policy, he asserted. Anticipating his detractors, he offered a document, signed by seventy-six members of the legislature and many other prominent Democrats, pledging their support for the amendment, their loyalty to the Democratic Party, and their assurance that the issue was not "a party question." As he neared the conclusion of his speech, Carroll's tone shifted away from that of a campaign brief to the vivid imagery of temperance literature and the pleading of an evangelical sermon: "Voices come to us from the graves of the lost. The tears of the sorrowing bedew our path," he exhorted. "The drunkard's widow in her poverty and the homeless orphan stretch out their pleading hands over the dark chasm." Carroll was preaching a civic sermon, calling sinners to repent and join a crusade.[18]

The response to Carroll's speech was swift and varied. Judge A.S. Broaddus wrote that although in his youth he had heard speeches by Henry Clay and Daniel Webster, he had never heard "such solid logic or such grandeur of eloquence as I heard fall from the lips of Rev. Dr. B.H. Carroll." But the antis were not so enthusiastic. Congressman Roger Q. Mills delivered a speech in which he asserted the prohibition movement was a northern import "brought in the bosoms of a Protestant political priesthood." He argued that "this government was not founded to protect and propagate Christianity at the cost of civil liberties," and that prohibition was simply that: an attack on personal liberty. "It was for liberty our forefathers bled, and for liberty they died," he declared, "and yet we are asked not to go and confess our enslavement to some self-constituted moral monster." Mills may have regretted his intemperate language. When approached for a copy of the speech for publication in the press, he reportedly replied that he had lost it. The version finally printed, and read by many Texas voters, was provided by the State Prohibition Executive Committee and their contracted stenographer. In the prohibitionist press Mills was accused of anticlericism and of siding with the "liquor manufacturers and the liquor dealers, the gamblers and the prostitutes . . . and the skeptics who hate religion," but the role of ministers of the gospel in the campaign once more was made a point of contention in the campaign.[19]

Preachers were not the only ones to take to the stump in support of prohibition. At the end of a prohibition convention at Fort Worth in late June, forty-nine men in attendance offered their services as speakers. Among them were a number of lawyers and judges, and several politicians including former U.S. Senator Samuel Maxey. The following week the Dallas *Daily Herald* announced the schedule of three speakers in that city, none of whom was identified as a clergyman. The San Antonio *Daily Express*, a decidedly anti-prohibitionist paper, followed the tour of Colonel Joel Miller, a local gentleman, and printed a favorable review despite its opposition to his cause. Through the summer, speakers visited nearly every community in the state. Larger towns hosted dozens. Local citizens held meetings or scheduled debates with visiting speakers. Some communities were overwhelmed. The citizens of Atlanta, Texas, voted to adopt a resolution offered by Rev. J.W. Erwin that they would "not recognize any self-appointed temperance lecturers, traveling through the country as a business, and taking up hat collections." And while not as numerous as their prohibitionist counterparts, antis, including a few prominent politicians, took to the stump in the hopes of defeating the amendment.[20]

Just as they had been in previous local option campaigns, the prohibitionists were wary of out-of-state allies. After the 1885 defeat in McLennan County, Texas prohibitionist leader James B. Cranfill wrote a letter to the editor of the New York *Voice* in which he pleaded with northern prohibition orators to stay away from the Texas fight. "We do not ask them to do this because of any prejudice we bear them," he wrote, "but we ask it in the interest of the cause we love so well." Even were Northerners to "come here with motives as pure as heaven" they could not avoid making the fight more difficult for Texas prohibitionists. He informed them that "the most potent argument our beloved Senator Coke used in his rum speeches last summer, was that Prohibition was of Northern origin, and foreign to Southern interests." Others were more willing to accept outside assistance. Prohibitionist Judge Robert West, who had already shown himself to be unorthodox on the issue of female speakers, defended the interlopers. Acknowledging that "some complaint has been made about Kansas men taking a hand," West asserted, "if a man has only been here two and a half hours he has a right to speak." When Kansas native Calvin Reasoner was criticized as an prohibitionist carpetbagger, he accused the antis of "waving the bloody shirt" to distract voters from the real issue in the contest. But opponents of the amendment kept up the attack on imported speakers. Barnett Gibbs conjured familiar demons when he decried the involvement of "short-haired women and long-haired men" in a speech early in the campaign. This regional xenophobia fueled political dirty tricks. The antis fabricated a prohibition pamphlet by taking out of context a press release from national Prohibition Party leader John B. Finch, in which he encouraged prohibitionists to vote anti-prohibition Democrats out of office. They reissued it under the headline "Prohibitionists of Texas, Heed the Call of Your Chief!" Recognizing the potential damage in affiliation with northern reformers, most prohibitionists were careful to emphasize that theirs was a local fight, unaffiliated with a national movement.[21]

In retaliation, prohibitionists could also point to outside interference in the campaign on the other side. The United States Brewers Association in convention at Baltimore voted to raise $5,000, and the National Association of Wholesale Liquor Dealers voted a 10-cent a barrel assessment on members, both to aid in the defeat of the amendment in Texas. Prohibitionists indignantly reprinted the stories. The Dallas *Daily Herald* printed a letter from the Anheuser-Busch Brewing Association instructing Texas anti-prohibitionists to bribe voters, particularly rural voters who were "more prone to be misled by fanatic parsons and meddling women." The same paper reported that twenty-five of the delegates to the Dallas anti-prohibitionist convention were from St. Louis. The editor could not prove that they were industry representatives, but suggested that they might be. "As to their exact mission we leave the public to draw their own conclusions," he wrote.[22]

The attack on interlopers were not the only evidence of prohibitionist efforts to authenticate their reform regionally. There was also an element of boosterism in much of the prohibition rhetoric. In this sense prohibition was a positive response to the uncertainty and disorder facing Texans in the decades following Reconstruction. The campaign reflected the extravagant hopes for the New South. "Let Texas lead in the van of the New South," urged S.A. Hayden of the *Texas Baptist and Herald.* "Let Texas get there first; then Tennessee and the others will follow. Texas leads the world." In another editorial he offered this prediction: "Give us prohibition in Texas and a half million of the best people in the older states will make our prairies bloom next year, and the prices of lands will double in less than five years." Hayden's enthusiasm swelled to postmillennial proportions. "The increased cultivation of the soil will superinduce regularity of rains and uniformity of seasons," he prophesied in the weeks prior to the vote. "Schools will flourish, churches will be multiplied and railroads like a network of steel will checker our fertile plains." The antis responded in kind, but their vision of a dry Texas was much bleaker. After lamenting the dearth of public celebration on San Antonio's plazas for Independence Day, the editor of the *Daily Express* observed that "nearly all the business houses were closed yesterday, the streets were deserted, and not a drunken man was in sight. In fact, it looked exactly like San Antonio will if prohibition goes into effect."[23]

Because so many editors took an early interest in the campaign, stump speakers did not need to draw large crowds to find an audience. Much of the campaign was conducted in the press. James B. Cranfill, editor of the Gatesville *Advance* (which he moved to Waco during the campaign), George W. Briggs of the *Texas Christian Advocate*, and S.A. Hayden of the *Texas Baptist and Herald* had urged the submission of the amendment, and devoted hundreds of column feet during the summer of 1887 to the campaign. Most of the state's urban daily papers opposed the amendment, but provided extensive coverage to the activities of both sides in the campaign. The Galveston *Daily News*, the only daily paper with a statewide circulation, vigorously opposed the reform but reported in detail on the various conventions and rallies of the prohibitionists, often printing major speeches. Support for the amendment came from the religious press and many of the smaller papers in the northern and eastern regions of the state. The Texas

WCTU established the *Cross Aider* in advance of the campaign, and Calvin Reasoner founded the *Texas Prohibition Advocate* with support from like-minded reformers. The Dallas *Daily Herald*, a staunchly prohibitionist paper, reported on the campaign in great detail, and on occasion would survey the journalistic landscape to report on competitors' coverage of the issue. In the early weeks of the campaign the *Herald* tallied the state's papers, finding out that of 176 newspapers in Texas, 129 had endorsed the amendment, 43 were opposed, and only 4 had yet to take a stand. At times the campaign dominated the news, particularly in the papers supporting prohibition. When B.H. Carroll penned "An Open Letter Interrogating the Chief Executive," taking Gov. Ross to task for his opposition to the amendment, the entire text, running nearly 5,000 words, was printed in full in at least two papers. Newspaper publishers often doubled as printers and promoters of campaign pamphlets, and provided critical publicity for such campaign literature as L.L. Pickett's "Hot Shot for the Whisky Demon," V.W. Grubbs' *Practical Prohibition*, and G.C. Rankin's *Two Nights in the Bar-Rooms and What I Saw There*. At least one editor, J.K. Street, of *Street's Monthly*, put down his pen and joined the campaign as a stump speaker.[24]

Despite their involvement in the campaign, the state's editors generally maintained collegial relations. In May the editors of the Dallas *Daily Herald* reported on the annual convention of the Texas Press Association in their city, and hosted a number of visiting editors at their offices. J.B. Cranfill ("the prohibition lightning striker") was as well received as Colonel Enoch Breeding ("the handsome and sedate True Blue of the Rockdale *Messenger*"), and the editor of the Houston *Anti-Prohibitionist* dropped by to pay his compliments. One break in the fraternal peace came when the Galveston *News* printed a criticism of the tactics used by George Briggs of the *Texas Christian Advocate*. Before the controversy was resolved, both Briggs and Hayden of the *Texas Baptist and Herald* were pressing for a boycott of the Galveston daily. The General Baptist Convention of Texas voted on a boycott of the paper in October of 1887, but the resolution was tabled after delegates J.B. Cranfill and R.T. Hanks, both prominent journalists, persuaded the convention to substitute a prayer offered by Major W.E. Penn for editors of the *News* that "they might be directed into right paths, might conduct the journal in a way to do good, and that they might all be saved finally in Heaven."[25]

While editors generally may have fully expected the furor created by the amendment campaign to boost readership, prohibitionist editors faced the possibility of decreased advertising revenues as a result of their opposition to the sale of liquor. In the early days of the campaign, before the editorial stance of the Dallas *Daily Herald* was clear, readers could find a full-page advertisement for Bell of Bourbon whisky on one page and on another an announcement that Dr. Hughes' Blackberry Cordial and Champagne Cider were offered "for sale by all druggists, grocers, and saloons" in the city. In subsequent issues these ads disappeared, and the editor reported that his paper was losing forty dollars a month as a result of his support of the amendment. Obviously the anti-prohibition press faced no such hardship; such stalwarts as the Galveston *News* and the San Antonio *Daily Express* continued to benefit from the sale of advertising space to brewers, distillers, and saloons. But the distinction was not always so clear in a time when the alcohol content of patent medicines, cordials, and tonics was uncertain. The staunchly prohibitionist *Texas Baptist and Herald* printed ads for the temperance elixir Compound Oxygen on the same page that it hawked Dr. Hughes' Blackberry cordial.[26]

The exhaustive coverage given the issue by the state's press provided voters with an extraordinary opportunity to study the issue of prohibition before casting a vote. Not every newspaper editor, preacher, politician, or stump speaker would address all aspects of the issue or present all sides fairly, but except in the most isolated rural areas of the state, it would be difficult for citizens to be unaware of the campaign and to avoid exposure to a considerable amount of analysis of the problems surrounding alcohol consumption and prohibition.

The social cost of alcoholic beverages was a central element of the campaign. Abused wives, neglected children, and ruined young men had become stock characters in temperance literature decades earlier, but they had real counterparts in many Texas families. Nevertheless, both prohibitionists and their opponents frequently abandoned the debate on drinking as an "intransitive vice" (today's "victimless crime"), and disputed instead the practicality of prohibition or the social cost of enforcement. Prohibitionists reprinted statistics on the per capita spending on alcohol and suggested that the money could better be spent on agriculture or manufacturing, and that even more would be saved from reducing expenses on "courts, prisons, and loss of labor." Antis respond that prohibition would dramatically reduce government revenues and would burden local economies with losses in rent and construction revenue. Prohibitionists cited the examples of Kansas and Atlanta, Georgia, where prohibition had been effective in reducing the incidence of public drunkenness and other crimes; antis countered that prohibition was unenforceable and that it encouraged disregard for the law. Prohibition would fail particularly "in Texas, where the population is scattered, requiring a vast expense to detect and punish violation of the law over a territory so extensive, and where the idea prevails that local sentiment rules in the locality even to the extent of ignoring the general law," the Galveston *News* predicted. "If it will not prohibit it will be a worse curse than universal drunkenness."[27]

The most effective, and most oft-repeated, attack on prohibition was the claim that the reform was an intolerable threat to personal liberty. Across the south white men in the years after Reconstruction were reasserting their social and political primacy by attacking any perceived threats to their liberty. African Americans, women, federal laws, even former slaveholders might scheme against the independence of the majority of white males. Prohibition was another attack on the independence and honor of white men. Antis accused prohibitionists of promoting sumptuary legislation and of jeopardizing the rights and responsibilities of individual citizens. "Prohibition is a concession to paternalism in government, which invites other concessions of like nature," Editor Jenkins of the Galveston *Daily News* warned. "Paternalism is inconsistent with the theory of personal liberty and individual responsibility." A San Antonio editor expressed similar fears: "When a man's house can be entered at pleasure by a sneaking informer . . . what has become of the declaration of independence, the constitution of the United States and the Jeffersonian democracy?" Prohibitionists dismissed these forebodings as demagoguery and on the stump and in print would refer to the argument as the "personal liberty dodge." Congressman Roger Mills, one of the most tireless expositors of the personal liberty argument, was lampooned as "Roger the Dodger." Nevertheless, in a region where white males bristled easily at threats to their sense of individual freedom, the argument proved an effective one for the antis.[28]

For white southern males in the latter decades of the nineteenth century, race was at the center of most public issues, and prohibition was no exception. Although black Texans often faced intimidation at local polls if they attempted to vote, or at least if they failed to vote the correct ticket, there had not yet been any systematic effort to disfranchise African Americans in the state. As a result the black vote would be a significant factor in the outcome of a statewide amendment vote. Both prohibitionists and antis appealed to black voters and enlisted prominent African Americans to aid their cause. In some instances every potential black voter in a community would be approached in advance and his pledge received to vote for or against the amendment, an overly scrupulous practice suggesting that coercion might be a factor. The *Texas Baptist and Herald* reported that of the one hundred black voters in Waxahachie, seventy-eight had signed "a pledge . . . to vote and work for the amendment."[29]

While there was some segregation in the organization of prohibition and anti-prohibition clubs at the precinct level, both sides generally welcomed African Americans in the audience at rallies, and black and white speakers often appeared on the same podium. A rally at Shady View Park in Dallas featured speeches by both white women and black men, a situation that would have been seen as intolerable in later years as southern whites became more obsessive about segregation. At a statewide anti-prohibition convention in May, a number of black orators addressed the audience at the suggestion of Barnett Gibbs. However, many events were not so well integrated. When Sallie Chapin of the South Carolina WCTU toured the state in support of the amendment she often spoke twice at each stop, once to a white audience and once to a black one.[30]

The separate organization of African American prohibitionist and anti-prohibitionist voters was not only a result of white racism. It occurred in part as a result of the initiative of African American leaders, particularly among the prohibitionists, who worked to generate support for the reform in their own community. They encouraged black voters to abolish the saloon that had tempted so many of them into a new form of slavery. I.W. Ferguson, president of the Colored Prohibition Club of Dallas was well received as a speaker. After hearing his address to an all-black audience at a rally, a correspondent for the Galveston *Daily News* reported that he "poured hot shot into the camp of the antis, and made a number of converts." On the other side of the issue, Melvin Wade, a black anti-prohibitionist, toured much of the state speaking to both mixed-race and segregated audiences. His itinerary was printed in several papers, and he received favorable reviews for his skillful oratory. At a time when many southern states were just beginning to experiment with new ways to restrict the political liberties of African Americans, black Texans on both sides of the prohibition debate were hosting picnics, organizing rallies, electing leaders, and mobilizing black voters to participate in the political process.[31]

Nevertheless, the prohibition campaign was not a color-blind affair. Southern whites had employed and would continue to employ racism as an effective element in political rhetoric. While both sides in the amendment fight recognized the importance of the black vote, each resorted to blatant stereotyping and racist attack when confronting African Americans on the opposite side of the issue. The *Texas Baptist and Herald* offered readers a mock sermon by a fictional black preacher, the Rev. Josaphat Gibbin. The piece was a glaring effort to ridicule those black clergy who were insufficiently supportive of the reform effort. After explaining Paul's admonition to Timothy to "take a little wine, for thy stomach's sake," the spurious cleric concluded, "Ef Paul says to Timothy, drink, that's enough for me; I'm goin' to drink." More frequently prohibitionists would express their confidence in the support of "the better class" of black voters, conceding the remainder to their opponents. At one point the press coverage of politically active African Americans turned particularly ugly when Melvin Wade was reported as having insisted that white "women be driven back to the wash tubs where they belong," rather than be allowed to speak publicly in support of prohibition. The inversion of racial stereotypes in his suggestion proved too threatening to the social order. The anti press denied that Wade had made the comment, but the prohibitionists were outraged and Wade's effectiveness as an antiprohibitionist orator was compromised.[32]

Two further incidents serve to illuminate the boundaries of the color line in the 1887 campaign. One highlights the limits of acceptable participation by African Americans in the campaign; the other demonstrates the point at which white racist rhetoric was deemed unacceptable and overly inflammatory.

Shortly after the opening of the prohibition campaign, B.H. Carroll received a letter from John B. Rayner, a Republican African American who had migrated to Robertson County from North Carolina in 1880. Rayner offered a number of suggestions for encouraging black Texans to support prohibition, including enlisting the support of the clergy of the African Methodist Episcopal Church and black editors. He also suggested inviting to Texas Bishop Henry McNeal Turner of AME church to tour the state in support of the amendment. He offered this advice in a letter to Carroll because he was "a prohibitionist from a deep religious principle and because the coming campaign will be fought on negroland, as the negro vote is quite an item and will play an important part in the coming election." He warned Carroll that the antis could buy votes among African Americans, and that the prohibitionists should move quickly to organize support in the black community.[33]

Carroll's efforts to enlist African Americans closely paralleled Rayner's suggestions, and when antis discovered and published Rayner's letter, there was a outcry over the influence of a black prohibitionist in the campaign. The clergymen and journalists that Rayner put forth as potential supporters did indeed become active in the campaign, and Bishop Turner left his home in Georgia to stump for the Texas amendment. The affair proved embarrassing to the white prohibitionist leader, who was "compelled to admit" the authenticity of the letter "before a crowd of 5000 people in Waco." Anti-prohibitionist speakers and editors ridiculed Carroll's willingness to follow the advice of an African American (however valuable it may have been), and accused the prohibitionists of "doing their utmost to catch the colored men in the traps prepared." The prohibitionists were vulnerable to accusations of trying to manipulate the black vote, and of doing so with the assistance of a black Republican.[34]

On the other hand, in their desire to attract the support of white voters, prohibitionists could employ stridently racist rhetoric, and anti-prohibitionists were willing to defend the political rights of African Americans when it served their purposes. A vituperative prohibitionist attack came from James Cranfill's Waco *Advance* in May, in an editorial entitled "The Native White Man," in which Cranfill recalled the trials of Reconstruction, just over a decade past. It had been a time "when the carpetbaggers, the bo-Dutchmen, and ignorant negroes [sic] ruled Texas." He warned his readers that the same "old radical carpet bag republican elements" were again threatening the sovereignty of the "native white Anglo-Saxon element of the South." He was confident that they would ultimately fail, because in the veins of the white Southerner "flows the blood of men unaccustomed to domination of any kind, and it will be a late day when they submit to having their institutions destroyed, their sacred days profaned, and their public buildings defaced by negroes and low-bred foreigners." Nevertheless, it behooved native southern white men to be vigilant. Cranfill accused the antis of depending on the political support of the "bo-Dutchmen and the ignorant buck nigger" to defeat the amendment. Equating support for prohibition with defense of white southern institutions, he declared that "native southern white men can be called to the support of the flag of their fathers." Cranfill's comments quickly became a target of the anti-prohibitionist press. In a prophetic editorial the San Antonio *Daily Express* predicted that should the prohibitionists gain control of the state government, they would "so hamper and annoy the colored men and foreign born citizens as to practically drive them out of politics, to disfranchise them by laws which, even if they would not stand the test of the supreme courts, would remain to harass and oppose those they intended to militate against through years of vexation before they could be stricken from the statute books." Of course many anti-prohibitionist politicians would support this very sort of disfranchisement in the future, but in 1887 they were looking to the black voter to assist them in the defeat of the amendment. And while many prohibitionists distanced themselves from Cranfill's language, there were more subtle ways to make the point. In a speech at Galveston the Rev. Atticus Haygood pointed to the advantages that black citizens had enjoyed under the post-Reconstruction southern governments. He admonished them to show their gratitude by supporting the amendment and "thus deserve further aid." Civil and political rights were contingent upon correct voting behavior.[35]

As Cranfill's attack in one breath on African Americans and German Texans demonstrates, partisans in the campaign did not always make fine distinctions of race and ethnicity. The German Texans were seen by prohibitionists, correctly, as staunch opponents to the amendment, and were often the subject of vehement attack. They drank beer publicly, they were often Catholic, and they or their parents were of foreign origin. The difficulty for the prohibitionists was the fact that the Germans were also perceived by most Texans as solid, respectable, middle-class citizens. They were a powerful political and social force in San Antonio and the Hill Country of Texas, and they could trace their Texas roots back farther than most of the xenophobic reformers. Germans had settled central Texas in the 1840s; many of the southern whites had not arrived until after the Civil War. One correspondent to the *Texas Baptist and Herald* summed up the prohibitionist dilemma when he described them as hardworking, industrious, and churchgoing, but also drinking, gambling, dancing, and heathen. Although they were for the most part "members of some so-called church," they did not appear to embrace the culture of the southern evangelical prohibitionists.[36]

The prohibitionists were correct in expecting that the Germans would oppose the amendment. San Antonio's Turner Hall was the site of numerous anti-prohibition rallies, sometimes conducted in German. Congressman William Crain, whose district encompassed much of the Hill Country, was a staunch opponent of the amendment. There was also a notable increase in citizenship applications from German immigrants in Texas cities in the weeks prior to the vote. The *Texas Baptist and Herald* printed the names of a number of applicants for citizenship. "These foreigners did not love the country sufficiently to accept naturalization before," S.A. Hayden wrote, "but when votes for whisky were to be cast, they are brought to the front." And while there were occasional reports of some German support for prohibition, there was no effort on the dry side to organize German voters. Jennie Bland Beauchamp, president of the Texas WCTU, appealed for assistance in supporting Baptist missionaries who would undertake "Gospel temperance work" among the German Texans, but she was not optimistic. "We can not do much for them until we get them from under the saloon influence," she wrote.[37]

Prohibitionists also expected the Mexican-American population of the southern counties to oppose the amendment. Balloting at the polls was public. The Anglo landholders, who generally opposed prohibition, could coerce or bribe tenants and employees to vote and could be sure that they voted as instructed. But it is also likely that few Tejanos would have supported the measure in the first place. One prohibitionist leader asserted, "on the Mexican border the plan has been let out to have a ball the night before the election, to get the Mexicans drunk; stay with them all night and march with them to the polls with tickets in their hands and vote for whisky." Antis did not dispute the accusation, but expressed concern that their efforts might be insufficient. Colonel Mac Anderson, on a speaking tour south from San Antonio to oppose the amendment, conceded that "as it takes a great deal of money to work up sufficient patriotism among Mexicans to get them to vote *en masse*," the turnout in the Valley would not be as substantial as the anti-prohibitionists would like.[38]

Prohibitionists often combined their hostility against non-Anglo voters with a nebulous class consciousness. Fannie Rees Pugh, of the Texas WCTU wrote to the *Union Signal* in March to complain that the greatest threat to the amendment would come from "nine hundred and ninety-nine negroes out of every thousand, the majority of the foreign population, and the rabble." Hayden of the *Texas Baptist and Herald* was equally harsh and imprecise in his criticism of the opposition: "The worst negroes, the least patriotic foreign element, the saloon men, the gamblers, the outlaws and the secret anarchists in our State . . . are for the perpetuation of the liquor traffic." Insofar as class distinctions are useful tools of analysis when dealing with an overwhelmingly rural state, it is likely that the amendment did enjoy more support from the middle-class professionals than from the population at large. The Dallas *Daily Herald* (which supported the measure) and the Galveston *News* (an anti paper) each conceded that the attorneys and physicians in the state tended to support the reform, and the *Texas Baptist and Herald* reported with satisfaction that the state teachers' convention had voted to support the amendment. On the other hand organized, and organizing, labor also appeared to provide some support for prohibition. The Austin Typographical Union voted overwhelmingly for a prohibition resolution, and the supporters of the amendment at the Workingmen's Hall in Dallas so frequently hosted prohibition rallies that the structure was rechristened "Temperance Hall" for the duration of the campaign.[39]

More important that the labor vote would be the farm vote in the August balloting. While rural counties were often the settings of the most successful efforts at local option prohibition, there was some concern about the willingness of Texas farmers to support the statewide ban. At the county level a number of Farmers' Alliances voted to support the amendment, but organizers of the Cotton Congress, made up of Alliance members from

Texas, Arkansas, and Louisiana, and held at Waco in May, opposed the measure. Organizers of the Texas Alliance scheduled a convention to begin August 2, and there were reports that the date had been selected so that farmers would be away from home at the time of the prohibition vote. Under pressure the leadership rescheduled the meeting. One correspondent to the *Texas Baptist and Herald* predicted that were farmers to turn out in great numbers, they would assure the success of the measure, but expressed concern that they might stay home because the issue might seem remote and unimportant in areas not yet penetrated by the "gilded saloon" and the "low dives." Nor could the prohibitionists take for granted the support of the more motivated rural voters. Barnett Gibbs discovered one farmer who planned to vote against the amendment "because it does not except liquor for agricultural purposes." What is certain is that both sides felt uncertain of the farm vote and worked to entice rural voters to the polls.[40]

Much of the bitterness in the campaign arose not from debates on the efficacy or wisdom of prohibition as public policy, but rather in the matter of the political orthodoxy of the reform. Since Democrats had regained control of the state government after Reconstruction, party leaders had worked to keep potentially divisive issues from threatening the party's hold on power. Important issues had been contested in elections: currency reform, subsidy and regulation of the railroads, fencing laws, and farm policy had all been subjects of public and legislative debate. Nevertheless, Democrats had worked with considerable success to keep these issues from deeply dividing the party at the crucial moments of conventions and elections.[41]

Prohibition was a more difficult issue, in great part because it already had a record at the local level. Voters had been expressing themselves in local option elections with increasing frequency since the adoption of the 1876 constitution, and the results were decidedly mixed. Democratic politicians had already taken public stands on the issue of prohibition at the local level, and their positions often put them at odds with their partisan colleagues in the legislature. So long as the issue remained a local one, however, there was no threat to party unity. Democrats in Jasper and Rockwall Counties could choose to outlaw saloons; those in Tarrant or Limestone could allow them; in Lamar County voters could change their minds every few years. The local policy had no bearing on the state party's agenda. In an effort to avoid a fight over the issue of statewide prohibition, the 1886 Democratic convention reaffirmed the party's commitment to the issue of local option, resolving that "every Democrat may indulge his own views without affecting his Democracy," but when supporters tried to force a resolution endorsing the submission of a prohibition amendment to the voters, their efforts ended in failure. Most Democrats would not risk their control of the state over such a potentially divisive issue.[42]

Individually, prominent politicians took diverse stands on prohibition. Senator Richard Coke, who had campaigned against the local option effort in McLennan County in 1885, stated that he would vote against the measure in August, but would not be active in the campaign. Senator John Reagan and former Senator Sam Bell Maxey worked on behalf of the amendment. Three of the state's congressional representatives publicly supported the measure. Governor Sul Ross, who was not a supporter, did not participate in the campaign, but former Governor John Ireland staunchly opposed the amendment. Former Lt. Governor Barnett Gibbs and Representative Roger Mills led the anti campaign. Whether they took a strong stand on one side or the other of the issue, or tried to remain aloof from the fray, politicians were accused of opportunism, and probably a number were looking ahead to the 1888 elections. But it is evident that within the political establishment, there was considerable divergence on the issue of prohibition.[43]

Despite the fact that many Democratic officeholders supported the amendment, the antis attacked the proposal as a challenge both to Democratic principles and to the party's political hegemony in the state. Rumors spread that the prohibitionists would run a full ticket of candidates in the 1888 state races should the amendment fail, a story that prohibitionists were quick to deny. A correspondent to the San Antonio *Daily Express* accused the prohibitionists of scheming to destroy both parties, an accusation backed up with excerpts from the National Prohibition Party's 1885 convention resolutions predicting the establishment of a third party in Texas. The anti-prohibitionists styled themselves the "True Blues," loyal to the party of the fathers, and the first statewide anti-prohibitionist convention was called in early May on behalf of True Blue Democrats across the state. A number of party leaders declined the invitation to attend, citing either support for the amendment or opposition to raising the issue of party loyalty. There was something of a backlash, with prohibitionist Democrats publicly rebuking and ridiculing their opponents. Appearing in June at a prohibition rally at Fort Worth, Senator Maxey told his audience, "I have been told that there was a little concern of a piebald description held in Dallas, which proposed to read me and Bonner, and Reagan, and Culberson, and Jarvis, and the great host of Democrats out of the party." Nevertheless, anti-prohibitionists, positioning themselves as champions of the Democratic Party, hoped to strike a chord with undecided voters who could be expected to put the interest of the party before the issue of the saloon.[44]

The campaign on both sides was waged in the public, face-to-face arena of nineteenth-century politics. Stump speakers debated local citizens on the podium or exchanged insults with hecklers in the audience, fraternal organizations held formal debates, saloons gave "complimentary balls," and both sides organized rallies, parades, and barbecues. The "Prohibition Mass Meeting" at Fort Worth in late June was attended by an estimated fifteen thousand people who filled over five acres of stands. After listening to speeches those in attendance lined up at over a mile of tables to feast on twenty-five head of cattle and over one hundred sheep and goats. To wash it all down an artesian well was dug and one contributor provided a 450-gallon tub of coffee, another supplied 300 gallons of iced tea. At Waco prohibitionists gathered and marched to Minglewood Park, where they listened to speakers, "after which a bounteous dinner was served by the ladies of Waco." At San Marcos a parade of decorated floats, accompanied by instrumental and vocal music led supporters to the Hays County prohibitionists' barbecue. The anti-prohibitionists at Fort Worth had pledges of "ten beeves for barbecue purposes" a month in advance of their rally, and the day before the event it was reported that "Panhandle cattlemen are donating beeves eight and ten at a time." The antis provided water, lemonade, tea, and coffee free of charge to those in attendance, and also advertised that they would sell "privileges" on the grounds. The morning of the Fort Worth rally, tens of thousands of participants from around the state began gathering and paraded to the grounds, accompanied by nine bands, including the Eighth Cavalry Band from San Antonio. Veterans headed the procession, carrying banners with portraits of Governor Sul Ross and Sam Houston. At dinner they were served 262 head of various livestock and 14,000 loaves of bread. Parallel, albeit smaller, events were held at Franklin, Cuero, Crockett, San Antonio, Brenham, Shepperd, Palestine, Killeen, Galveston, and just about anywhere a crowd could be gotten up to listen to speeches and to feast. Some were organized jointly by the prohibitionists and the antis, with formal debates scheduled before and after the food. The most publicized of these joint events was a debate at Waco on July 6 between Representative Roger Mills and the Rev. B.H. Carroll. The two leaders met before a crowd of seven thousand gathered at Padgitt's Park, and the full text of their speeches was published in newspapers throughout the state.[45]

In the last days before the August 4, 1887 vote, Texas was ablaze with torchlight processions, bonfires, and barbecues as both sides in the campaign worked to get out the vote. At Fort Worth partisans held meetings at three different locations on August 2; at Brownwood both the antis and the pros held barbecues and torchlight parades in the last two days of the campaign; at San Antonio many businesses were closed for three days prior to the vote, and almost all merchants closed their doors on election day. The evening before the election San Antonio voters could choose to hear speeches at one prohibition and two anti rallies, or march in procession for or against the amendment. At Willis the two camps held simultaneous barbecues in different parts of town and each drew over two thousand people. At Sherman over a thousand marched in parade led by the Paris Cornet Band, a drum corp, and a number of floats and carriages. Waco hosted two parades, one for the pros and one for the antis, and at the following prohibition rally two speakers spoke simultaneously at opposite ends of the grounds, one to white voters and one to black. It appeared as if every Texan with any stake at all in the outcome of the vote was on the streets, on a podium, or at a pulpit on the eve of the election.[46]

On the morning of Thursday, August 4, most retail establishments in Texas were closed. Those that sold alcohol, which in addition to the saloons would have included most drug stores and grocers, were closed by order of the Attorney General. It would have been difficult to find a wagon or a carriage for hire anywhere in the state. Activists on both sides had booked them in advance to transport voters to the polls. County commissioners selected precinct polling sites, but in most counties voting would take place at schools, government offices, or stores. Voters could obtain ballots in advance, but when placed in the box all ballots had to be marked by hand for or against the various amendments. The law required that on the question of prohibition the voter must mark either "For State Prohibition" or "Against State Prohibition" to cast a valid vote. Any variation would render the ballot void. There was no guarantee of or provision for secrecy in balloting, and the election judge presiding might at his discretion read aloud ballots as they were cast. In the cities and larger towns, particularly those with active WCTU chapters, women in the community set up tables and offered refreshments and last-minute exhortation to voters as they came in. Stronger drink would be discreetly available at most polling places courtesy of the antis.[47]

There was a great deal of forecasting in the days before the vote, prohibitionists generally expecting that they would carry the day and the antis predicting that the amendment would be soundly rejected. Even in counties that had never voted dry in local option elections, prohibitionists were confident that their efforts through the summer had swayed enough voters to pass the measure, and that they had countered successfully the anti-prohibitionist accusations that prohibition was the creation of northern radicals.

Anticipating the passage of the amendment five weeks before the vote, editor Hayden of the *Texas Baptist and Herald* wrote, "the Prohibition campaign in Texas is evidently destined to be far more closely contested and exciting than any of those in which the Republicans and Democrats as such confronted each other." The Galveston *Daily News*, predicted that the number of votes cast would be greater than in any previous election in the state, and that true Southerners would reject the amendment handily. Both editors were correct about the intensity and level of participation in the campaign. Texans would shortly know who had correctly called the results. The reader may wiat a bit longer. However, before surveying these results, it would be helpful to undertake a close examination of the southern strategy of the campaign as it spilled over into violence in the weeks prior to the vote.[48]

The Alamo, ca. 1880's

Courtesy of the Daughter of the Republic of Texas Library, CN95.44

Chapter 4

"The Blood of the Mighty Dead Has Stained Me!"[1]

Eggs and Honor in the 1887 Campaign

Like their allies to the north and east, the prohibitionists of Texas believed with considerable justification that their reform was a worthy and noble cause. Alcohol took its toll in nineteenth-century America, and those few individuals who had no firsthand knowledge of the costs of alcohol abuse could find evidence enough in the popular press. Temperance had played a central role in American reform before the Civil War; its revival after that great conflict has been attributed to a variety of developments. Historians have pointed to the growth of cities, the fear of immigrants, and the need of industrialists for a more sober and compliant work force as factors contributing to the reemergence of temperance.

In the southern states, these explanations seem inadequate. Certainly there were parallels. Saloons were a problem in southern cities, immigrants did often drink, and aspiring industrialists, particularly in the southern railroads, did want sober workers. But urbanization, immigration, and industrialization were not the prevailing features of the South.

There is a religious element that parallels the northern experience and provides a simple explanation of the popularity of prohibition. Temperance was an evangelical cause in every region, and the support for the measure among southern Methodists and Baptists mirrors the support given the cause by their brethren in the North. But before the war Southerners had been wary of religious reformers, and had even restricted the political activities of the clergy. Abolitionism, after all, had evangelical roots. In the eighteenth century white southern evangelicals had been critical of slavery and their critique of the system was viewed as dangerous and incendiary. Eventually, they made their peace with slavery. Criticism was muted, and finally transformed into a defense of the system. Slaveholders were converted, and evangelicals acquired slaves. The southern states only became the Bible Belt after evangelicals embraced many of the core values of white southern society.[2]

Temperance had not been among those core values, but neither was it a threat to the power structure. A recently converted relative who criticized holding human beings as property was a revolutionary; one who refused a drink of whisky was merely an eccentric. But while eccentrics might be tolerated, they hardly could hope to remake society. Prohibitionists needed to reposition themselves in the ideological mainstream. If they were going to reform the South, they must first demonstrate their own regional authenticity.

Critics of prohibition had pointed out that they stood outside the mainstream of white southern society in two essential ways. First, there was a simple *ad hominem* argument that prohibitionists were interlopers. The prohibitionist was a meddlesome carpetbagger, and merited the same respect as did any other northern opportunist. The second attack was ideological and political: Whatever the nativity of its proponents, prohibition was a northern reform, akin to abolitionism, racial egalitarianism, or congressional Reconstruction. However well meaning its proponents may be, prohibition was a decidedly un-southern idea.

Prohibitionists defended themselves on both fronts. They minimized the role of outsiders in their campaign. Prohibitionists would be as southern and as Texan as their opponents. Ideologically, they looked for the southern roots of their reform. They avoided connection with the national prohibition movement, and they worked to place prohibition squarely within the particular historical development of the region and the state.

One incident in particular serves to illuminate the issue. Two months before the vote on the amendment, prohibition speakers were pelted with eggs at a rally in San Antonio. A firestorm of debate erupted throughout the state in the wake of the attack. The ensuing debates over the honor, the motives, and the origins of the various participants in the scandal provided an opportunity for prohibitionists to assert the regional authenticity of their cause. For most Texan prohibitionists the goal was not to enact national prohibition, with Texas as one step along the way. Theirs was a crusade to fashion a particular kind of society in a particular place. The prohibitionists were creating a new Texas, piecing together elements of traditional white southern culture and Anglo-Texas history.

A crowd that would number close to three thousand had begun gathering on the government lot between Avenues D and E across from Alamo

Plaza late in the afternoon for the prohibition meeting scheduled for the evening of June 7, 1887. One of the featured speakers, Bishop Henry McNeal Turner of the African Methodist Episcopal Church, had recently arrived in San Antonio from Atlanta, and was engaged in a brief tour of Texas in support of the prohibition amendment. Earlier in the afternoon several wagons that would serve as the speakers' platform had been driven over to the lot by members of one of the local AME congregations, but they had been dispersed by Officer P.J. Burgin, who said he was acting under the orders of the city marshal. Instead, packing crates were drawn together in one corner of the lot and draped with a prohibition banner.[3]

The local prohibition committee had applied four days earlier to the city council for the use of Alamo Plaza for their meeting, but the council had voted that it could allow the meeting only with the consent of the mayor. Mayor Bryan Callaghan demurred, arguing that he could not guarantee the safety of those participating in a prohibition rally given the hostility of the great majority of the town's citizens to the proposed amendment. The prohibitionists had also considered hiring Turner Hall, the meeting place of a prominent German-American organization, but the Turner Association had resolved that "the prohibitionists should not have the use of Turner hall either for love or money." The meeting was then moved to the nearby vacant lot recently purchased by the federal government for the construction of the new federal offices in town.[4]

Long before the featured speaker arrived the crowd began to grow noisier, and it was soon clear that most were not there to support the prohibitionists' efforts. A number of policemen were patrolling the perimeter of the crowd to watch for signs of violence, and at the northern edge of Alamo Plaza a group of prominent citizens had gathered, including Mayor Callaghan, Bexar County Sheriff Nat Lewis, and City Marshal Philip Shardein.

As darkness began to fall oil lamps were lighted and held aloft by four men at the corners of the platform, brightly illuminating the makeshift stage, but casting light only a few yards into the swelling crowd that pushed closer to where the speakers would stand. Just after nine o'clock W.H. Brooker of the state prohibition committee mounted the platform and began waving his arms to try to quiet the crowd so that he might introduce Bishop Turner. His voice was drowned out entirely in the catcalls and hisses of his audience and he quickly abandoned his efforts. The Rev. A.F. Jackson of a local AME church then stepped up on the platform, but was no more successful in quieting the crowd than Brooker had been. Finally Bishop Turner mounted the platform and tried to begin his speech without an introduction. He too was shouted down and after a few minutes he gave up and stepped down.

At this point there could be heard from the crowd calls for "Lockwood." Arthur Lockwood was the proprietor of the Star and Crescent Saloon and Billiard Parlor, and at one time had served as an alderman. He was standing near the platform and when his name was called he waved to the crowd. With apparent reluctance he climbed on the boxes to speak. The noise subsided as he began, first apologizing to the prohibitionists for using their platform and lights. He then launched into a speech of his own, castigating the prohibition committee and condemning the proposed amendment as an attack on personal liberty. By the time he concluded and descended from the platform the crowd was again shouting. As Lockwood stepped down one side of the platform Rev. A.H. Sutherland climbed the other. Sutherland was a local Methodist minister who traveled extensively in the southern portion of the state addressing audiences in English and Spanish in support of the prohibition amendment. As he began to address the crowd an egg flew from the vicinity of the Maverick homestead at the western edge of the lot and struck Sutherland over his left eye. It was reported that other eggs were thrown, and that Sutherland, a man named McClure, and by some accounts the Bishop himself were struck several times. Sutherland later suggested that his ordeal be remembered as the second battle of the Alamo. "For half an hour the missiles flew, the storm raged and the thunders shook the very earth at every attempt of that native born Texan to speak and that on the very ground bought and baptized by Sutherland blood." Indeed his recollection of the event was already the stuff of myth:

> The question now rapidly arose to the magnitude of eternal truth. Gory forms were seen starting from their resting places, while every stone of the Alamo cried out, "The blood of the mighty dead has stained me!" Prohibition and anti-prohibition, individualities and personalities were lost sight of while the angel of the covenant stretched forth his hand and saved the day. The slain of the Lord were many.

Sutherland reported that he had been "determined to face and fight the infuriated mob to the bitter end, and, had not the torch bearers marched away he would have conquered a peace or cleared the field." As it was, the entire prohibition delegation retired to the church that was hosting Bishop Turner and continued their speeches there.[5]

Editors across the state quickly decried the event as an outrage. Even those strongly opposed to the prohibition amendment moved quickly to condemn the mob. The San Antonio *Daily Express* declared "the assault on Rev. Mr. Sutherland was detestable, cowardly in the lowest degree of cowardice, and was incited by that vilest of combinations, bigotry, intolerance, insolence and lawlessness, and no effort should be spared to ferret out the perpetrators, as well as the ring leaders in the riot, and punish them to the fullest extent of the law." Indeed two men were arrested shortly after the incident and convicted of assault. John Young was described as a "colored barber"; M. Seelas was an employee of the Lone Star Brewery. Each was assessed a fine of fifty dollars and jailed in default of payment; Seelas was fired from his position at the brewery.[6]

The furor over the event escalated dramatically later in the week when W.H. Brooker submitted an affidavit to the federal district court in which he told his version of the story. Based on Brooker's account a deputy United States marshal arrested the mayor, the city treasurer, the city marshal, and several others on Friday, June 10, on a charge of conspiracy to commit aggravated assault. The business of the city ground to a halt as U.S. Commissioner James Stevenson of the western district of Texas heard several days of testimony from participants in and witnesses to the scandalous affair. The accounts was contradictory and inconclusive, and the city fathers were eventually released with no action taken, but the "rotten egg business" in San Antonio became a lightning rod in the prohibition campaign until after the vote in August.

At first glance, it is not an easy thing to explain why both prohibitionists and their opponents were so overwrought by the egging of prohibition speakers. No one suffered serious injury, and prohibitionists had endured greater ignominies for their efforts for decades. Nevertheless, the assault on the prohibition speakers in San Antonio was the occasion for vituperative attacks from the prohibition and religious press and earnest soul-searching on the part of anti-prohibitionists. The editor of the Kerrville *Eye*, no partisan of prohibition, proclaimed, "the curs who throw rotten eggs at public speakers have hearts as putrid and defunct [sic] as the eggs they throw." But there was more at stake here than the reputations of those who hurled the eggs. The San Antonio *Daily Express* expressed the fear that even in such an anti-prohibition city the attack on the prohibitionist speakers would galvanize support for the amendment. Public outrage was such that the editor lamented that the amendment would have passed by "a good round majority" in that otherwise decidedly anti-prohibition city had it been put to a vote in the week following the incident.[7]

Whatever their position on the prohibition issue, observers of the incident in San Antonio were in agreement on two things. First, the attack on the speakers was an assault upon their honor; second, the perpetrators showed themselves dishonorable and worthy of nothing but contempt. Anti-prohibitionists hoped that by quickly acknowledging the affront (and by placing blame on a few individuals clearly outside the bounds of honorable behavior) the prohibition cause would not receive a long-term boost from the incident. The prohibitionists, on the other hand, viewed the assault as characteristic of their opponents. Prohibition was an honorable cause and its enemies acted dishonorably. The facts of the case might be subject to dispute, but there was a consensus on the necessary resolution. There must be an appropriate response to aggrieved honor.

This concern on both sides of the issue with honor is important to an understanding of the context of the prohibition campaigns in Texas. Throughout the history of the temperance movement, its advocates had been portrayed by their opponents as radicals and cranks. In the Texas campaign they had been disparaged as "long-haired men and short-haired women." As such they could be dismissed as ridiculous and generally harmless. But the prohibitionists also faced a more serious charge. They were accused of being the dupes of northern reformers, engaged, unwittingly perhaps, in an attack on southern institutions and values. However, if the incident provided a clear indication that Sutherland, and by extension the prohibitionists generally, more closely followed the dictates of an honor code, then the prohibitionists could claim to be the true exemplars of southern society.[8]

Observers of southern behavior have since the early nineteenth century commented on the Southerner's obsession with honor. Anyone familiar with the speeches and editorials of southern politicians and writers, particularly in the years immediately preceding the Civil War, could not be unaware of the frequency to which southerners appealed to honor to explain their grievances and subsequent behavior. Nevertheless, the importance of honor in southern culture is a troublesome matter. Part of the difficulty arises from a problem of definition. Southern honor, historian Edward Ayers writes, "was simultaneously potent and elusive." Anthropologists, social scientists, and historians have all grappled with the concept. Nevertheless, it is clear that Southerners took the notion of honor very seriously. Despite the tumultuous changes in the political and social structure of their region in the decades following the Civil War, many white Southerners found considerable resonance in the code of honor, and saw their region as particularly rich in its virtues.[9]

In simple terms, a code of honor in a society serves two basic functions. First, it distinguishes between those members of society who are worthy of honorable treatment from those who are not. Second, it establishes the rules of behavior for those within the honor group. An honorable individual has the right to expect that others will treat him with due respect, deference, or regard. A person's honor is also a right to be jealously guarded. It is not unalienable; it can be lost if it is not properly defended. Particular actions— an assault or an attempt to humiliate or to discredit—can serve to undermine the individual's claim to the right to honorable regard. If the prohibitionists understood honor in this sense, then the egging incident posed extraordinary dangers. Not only were the egg throwers acting dishonorably, but they were placing in jeopardy the honor of their intended targets. Moreover, they jeopardized the cause itself. If Sutherland accepted this attack on his honor then the anti-prohibitionists would be justified in claiming that his was not a truly honorable (and not a truly southern) cause at all.[10]

It works this way: Rev. Sutherland had ample cause to expect the respect and deference of his audience. He was a prominent cleric in San Antonio and was engaged in what he and many other prominent Texans regarded as a crucial political battle. More importantly on this particular occasion, he was also the descendant of Sutherlands who had fought in the Texas Revolution, Sutherlands who had sacrificed blood (but not honor!) in the primordial events of his culture. By throwing eggs at him, his assailants jeopardized his claim to that dignified status. The eggs were more devastating than the musket balls fired at his forefathers.

Certainly the intensity of Sutherland's response to the event supports this interpretation. Significantly, so do the responses of all other commentators on the event. Prohibitionists lashed out at the assailants and demanded satisfaction for Sutherland. The antis grieved less for Sutherland, but were at least as damning in their attacks on the egg throwers. The editor of the San Antonio *Daily Express* called the prohibition cause "an outrage upon the citizen," but declared the attackers guilty of "brutal violence and loud-mouthed blackguardism and blasphemy." This was no small matter.[11]

The ambiguous role of Bishop Turner in the event highlights the dilemma faced by prohibitionists in their efforts to view the egging in the context of southern honor. African American voters represented a potentially critical constituency for the reformers and their opponents, and it was unclear how they would vote. As a result, both prohibitionists and anti-prohibitionists stumped for the votes of black Texans. However each did so cautiously. Allowing African Americans too prominent a role in the campaign could alienate potential white supporters. And when the event was transformed from one of many prohibition rallies to a contest of honor, Turner's presence became all the more problematic for the prohibitionists. As an African American, Turner, in the eyes of the white participants, could not claim a right to honorable treatment at the hands of the crowd. Furthermore, his association with the event potentially could have diminished Sutherland's claim. As a result Turner virtually disappeared in the prohibitionist accounts of the incident. In the prohibition press editorials that followed, it was only Sutherland whose honor had been assaulted.[12]

The omission of the role of Bishop Turner in most accounts of the incident does not mean that as an African American Turner was unworthy of attention. After all, for their part prohibitionists had embraced Bishop Turner as an ally in the cause. He was regarded as an effective advocate to the black voters of Texas who might support prohibition. And as a symbol of the respectable black citizen he aided the prohibition cause. On the one hand his status as a church leader helped to disarm critics who might ridicule the prohibitionists for allying themselves with socially inferior African Americans. On the other hand he offered a rebuttal to the charges that prohibitionists were simply trying to take away rights given to African Americans at the end of the Civil War. His role in the prohibition campaign itself was significant. Nevertheless, Bishop Turner disappeared because as an African American he had no place in an affair of southern honor.[13]

The Rev. Sutherland's foremost concern was his personal honor as it is viewed by those within his honor group, white southern males. It was crucial for the legitimacy of the prohibition cause that his honor be respected. If he were treated with the respect that his status accorded him, then by association his cause merited respect also. If the prohibitionists were honorable white southern males with all the rights and privileges that this designation implies, then prohibition was a legitimate policy because it sprang from authenticated southern roots.

Because it drew upon powerful and venerable themes deeply imbedded in southern culture, the Texas prohibition campaign reflected another concern of southern whites—the legacy of slavery. During the secession crisis of the 1850s, Southerners were hypersensitive to threats to their freedom and viewed a variety of political developments from nullification through the Wilmot Proviso to the election of Lincoln as efforts to enslave them. There was a necessary convergence of the white male Southerner's obsession with his honor and his freedom. He believed that only free men could lay claim to honor. As a result insults to honor were viewed as real attacks upon liberty, and challenges to political power (i.e., the sanction of political freedom) were viewed as affairs of honor.[14]

This convergence of liberty and honor placed the white Southerner in a vulnerable position. Military defeat in the Civil War and the humiliation of Reconstruction did not force an abandonment of the code of honor, but it necessitated a new defense. Defeat in battle was not dishonorable if one fought courageously, nor did honor require a blatant refusal to comply with Reconstruction policies. And like the southern regard for honor, the importance of freedom did not disappear with military defeat and the emancipation of the slaves. In fact, with the abolition of slavery and the erasure of the legal sanction to distinguish between slave and free, Southerners were especially wary of threats to their liberties.[15]

Central to the prohibition campaign was the so-called "personal liberty argument." For the anti-prohibitionists, prohibition was "sumptuary legislation" that impinged on the liberty of free individuals to determine their own behavior. Hundreds of speeches and articles were published outlining the case against imposing unnecessary restrictions on the recreation of free men. The issue was just as compelling to the prohibitionists, and they devised an alternative interpretation of the personal liberty argument. In their view the saloon enslaved free men; real personal liberty came only with the destruction of the "liquor interests." Even more telling, they criticized their political opponents as slaves to the saloon interests, politicians who were not free to vote their consciences or in the interests of their constituents. And because they had willingly relinquished their freedom, these politicians could not be expected to conduct themselves honorably.[16]

It is in this regard that the prohibitionists' accusations directed toward political leaders in San Antonio are particularly significant. According to the official, and anti-prohibitionist, version of the event, the assault was the action of a few individuals who, regrettably, could not be expected to conduct themselves according to the code of honor because of their race or social position. If, however, as the prohibitionists maintained, the assault had the sanction of the leaders of the community, then the honor of any anti-prohibitionist was questionable. Even if the city officials did not participate directly in the egging, their inability or unwillingness to stop it demonstrated a dereliction of duty, and a violation of the code of honor which demanded that one perform one's duty at all costs. That, according to one witness who testified at the U.S. Commissioner's hearing, was exactly what had happened. Dr. P.W. Johns reported that Mayor Callaghan "was laughing excessively" at the plight of the speakers and "seemed to be enjoying the sport pretty much." Worse than that, when a "little German" asked the mayor if he intended to do anything to control the crowd, the mayor responded, "if the people want to halloa, I can't help it; I can't keep them from it. I don't care a damn how much they holloa; you speak as if you think we are entirely to blame for this thing; go to the devil, will you." And while Commissioner Stevenson concluded at the end of the proceedings that there was not sufficient evidence to proceed with criminal charges, when the hearings recessed each day he refused to release the potential defendants on their own recognizance, requiring from each a $100 bond. This action, with its implication that the city fathers would not honor their pledge to appear in court, made headlines in the next day's paper.[17]

While the code of honor emphasized, paradoxically, both freedom and duty for white men, for women there was less equivocation. Certainly, honor demanded the chivalrous treatment of women in social relations, but it also led to an extraordinary concern for the sexual purity of females. As a result, prohibition was often portrayed as a means to protect the women of Texas. The supporters of the saloon "send the demon of intemperance into happy homes," according to the Committee on Address and Resolutions of the Dallas County Prohibition Convention. The prohibitionists, on the other hand, "shield the loving wife . . . from the inflictions of the fiery fiend." The editor of the *Texas Baptist and Herald* condemned the "liquor men" who were "trying to persuade the honest citizens of Texas to vote the homes of the mothers of Texas desolate and sell the honor of the State."[18]

Of course the sentiment expressed in this appeal differs little from similar declarations of northern temperance advocates. Both northern and southern women could be the victims of the brutality or financial ruin of drunken husbands. And yet the language of the Texas newspapermen reflected a distinctive, regional emphasis. When an anti-prohibition paper had criticized women stump speakers in the campaign, the state Baptist newspaper, while skirting the issue of women speaking in public, responded that "the honor of our Southern manhood was shocked by this unchivalrous slur upon our countrywomen."[19]

A clearer regional distinction was evident when the appeal to honor highlighted the white southern male's concern with female sexual purity. And redress for honor threatened could be disturbingly racist and particularly brutal when the purity of southern womanhood was at stake. Prohibition was necessary, the argument went, so that black men would not get drunk and rape white women. When the state of Tennessee was debating a model saloon license law, H.M. Du Bose, who had been the pastor of a church in Texas several years earlier, reported his experience in the Texas campaigns. He had been a leader of the efforts to close the saloons in his community, but a local option effort was defeated when "a man, claiming to be a democrat . . . conduct[ed] to the polls a horde of vagabond negroes, corralled on his own premises in the town, and [stood] over them while they voted to kill my own and the other respectable votes of the town." As a result "a negro habitue of one of these dives, which I had sought to wipe out, assaulted the wife of a young farmer some miles from the town, outraged her person, and ripped her dead body with a fifteen-cent jackknife." The community's response was swift, and, in the mind of the minister, more appropriate than any police action. "The next day the brute was captured, tied to a stake within fifty feet of the door of the dive that made him, and was burned to death in the presence of five thousand people," he reported. "After that the town came to its senses and voted the saloons out." The result was that "rape and outrage have fallen off fifty per cent since prohibition began to prevail in the south." There was, in Du Bose's mind, a seamless transition from a murderous lynch mob avenging dishonor to a citizenry enacting legislation. The latter action might render the former less necessary, but they served the same cause.[20]

Personal courage (in contrast to an opponent's cowardice) was another element of a code of honor that played prominently in the reporting of events surrounding the campaign. When Roderick Dhu Gambrell, whose father would later become the editor of the Texas *Baptist Standard* and a leader in the prohibition campaigns, was gunned down, apparently as a result of his role in the prohibition efforts in Jackson, Mississippi, the editor of the *Texas Baptist and Herald* eulogized him:

> Now here was a young man, 23 years old, poor, moneyless, with nothing but his character for honor, honesty and a manly courage, and against him was pitted a prominent political leader, with ample fortune and high position, and yet with all these odds against the youth, he so far convinced the honest people of Hinds county of the justice of his cause as to the defeat this whisky champion, for which he was brutally murdered from the coward's hiding place.

When "gentlemen offered to take the field" as stump speakers for the cause they would often recall the glorious death of Roderick Gambrell.[21]

It is one thing for a southern journalist to be cast in the role of a fallen knight; it should be quite another for a clergyman like Sutherland to take the field. In western European societies, the clergy (along with actors, prostitutes, and scholars) were traditionally excluded from the dominant honor group. Southern evangelicalism in particular, with its fierce individualism and Protestant anthropology of spiritual egalitarianism, should be anathema to a community-based ethic of hierarchy, personal loyalty, and violence. Indeed, evangelical Protestants from colonial times were consistent critics of many elements of southern culture which historians have linked to the code of honor. Drunkenness, gambling, dueling, and later lynching were often subject to the scrutiny and wrath of evangelical divines, leading historians to argue that evangelicalism had a corrosive effect on the place of honor in southern culture.[22]

Certainly there is considerable dissonance in the coexistence of southern evangelicalism and southern honor. At times this dissonance could strike at the very heart of southern society. Still, it is important to recognize another fact: It was quite possible for individuals in southern society to hold, alternately or simultaneously, to both sets of values. Evangelicals in the South began as critics of the slaveholding elites, but despite their egalitarian theology, as the nineteenth century progressed and as they entered the upper ranks of southern society, they muted their criticism, and appropriated that rank's view of the social order.[23]

In his testimony before the U.S. Commissioner's court following the San Antonio incident the Rev. Sutherland alluded to the difficulty of balancing his role as a man of honor and a man of the cloth. Although he had written to the editor of a local paper about his determination to "face and fight the infuriated mob to the bitter end," and to "[conquer] a peace or clear the field," his actions betrayed a more complex frame of mind. When he was finally forced from the speaker's platform, he was approached by Gus Kampmann, owner of Kampmann's Sash, Door, and Blind Factory and the son of a wealthy banker. Kampmann made a personal and unmistakable assault on the minister's honor. Kampmann "began to curse him bitterly and took [Sutherland's] hat off and hit it down on his head." It was a difficult thing for a man of honor to suffer curses passively. But an assault on one's hat was perhaps an even more odious affront. The wearer of a hat indicated his respect by removing his hat. Conversely, failure to remove one's hat could be regarded as an indication that those present did not merit the honor. A white southern male would remove his hat upon entering the home of a white family; he would leave it on his head in a black home. Kampmann attacked the blazon of Sutherland's status as a gentleman, and it placed the clergyman in a very awkward position. Sutherland felt compelled to explain that "he felt at one time inclined to thrash Kampmann, which he was perfectly able to do, but his principle and calling prevented him."[24]

Other clerics were not so restrained by internalized checks on their impulse to heed the code of honor. James B. Cranfill, a physician, minister, and long-time editor of prohibitionist and religious papers, recalled an event from his early adulthood in Texas. He had been in his office in Gatesville one afternoon when he heard a gunshot from the direction of the courthouse. Without hesitation he grabbed a pistol and started for the door. "I did not know whether or not some of my friends were involved," he reported, "and if there is any virtue whatsoever in the western man, it is that of fidelity to his friends under any and all conditions." He was stopped at the door by his father who was visiting. He acknowledged that his father was correct in preventing him from getting involved in the fight, but only after discovering that he did not know the combatants well. Had they been friends he would have been honor-bound to join their ranks whether or not they had instigated the fray.[25]

Cranfill recognized that "the Northern and Eastern reader will wonder how a man could be a Sunday School teacher and at the same time carry a 45 Colt revolver in his hip pocket." He does not elaborate, except to conclude the narrative with another story, this one concerning Captain Bill McDonald of the Texas Rangers. McDonald, too, had been a Sunday School teacher. One Sunday morning he was called out to investigate a report of horse theft. He was able in short order to track down the suspects, but met with resistance when he tried to arrest them. "The result was that when the smoke of battle cleared away, four of the Mexicans were dead," Cranfill recounted. "The officer had done his duty, and it was still time for Sunday School, so Captain McDonald hastened back to the little frontier meeting house and opened his Sunday School as usual." Neither Cranfill nor McDonald saw any difficulty in reconciling a call to martial duty with a call to preach the gospel. Both were honorable callings.[26]

Despite the occasional involvement of prominent African American clergy and educators such as Bishop Turner, most of the Texas prohibitionists were white Southerners. The leadership in the 1887 campaign included ministers and lay leaders of southern evangelical churches, editors of religious newspapers, and politicians with close ties to the evangelical churches. Most were born in the older states of the former Confederacy, some having participated in the movement prior to moving to Texas. They shared with other late nineteenth-century reformers a deep suspicion of aliens and trusts, but with only a few exceptions they were not radical reformers, anti-capitalists, or even populists. They drew instead on what they perceived as conservative cultural values. They were at least as likely as their opponents to reject the "meddling" of distant corporations or federal officers. They were not always so reactionary as to eschew New South boosterism, but they consciously employed what they perceived as timeless, community-based values of the Old South. Prominent among these was honor.[27]

In addition to frequent references to the honor of individuals in the prohibition campaigns, there is an abiding concern with what anthropologist Julian Pitt-Rivers refers to as "collective honor." In the Texas prohibition campaigns, a sense of collective honor often took the form of conventional southern regionalism. A Baptist paper warned that it was a "stain on the honor of Texas to vote under the dictates of Northern liquor men." Prohibitionist speakers and editors from the beginning had to establish their impeccable southern credentials. To be from as far north as Kansas, that hotbed of unionism, would make a prohibitionist a liability to his own party.[28]

Frequently, however, a sense of collective honor was more evident in the reverent treatment of artifacts, heroes, or myths of Texas history. By linking their campaign with Texas Revolution the prohibitionists cloaked themselves in the honor of familiar heroes. The assault on Sutherland, after all, had taken place on hallowed ground. When Prohibition Committee Chairman B.H. Carroll was warned that he would not be safe speaking in San Antonio, he responded that "he intended to speak in the shade of the Alamo, where Crockett, Travis, and Bowie fell, and if need be, like those heroes take his life in his own hands."[29]

The battle of the Alamo, which provided the vivid backdrop for Rev. Sutherland's vision, had already been established as the natal event in Anglo-Texas mythology. It had been eagerly appropriated by southern evangelicals who hoped to impose a new moral order on what they saw as a lawless, godless society. Rufus C. Burleson, president of the new Baptist college at Waco (which the Dallas *Daily Herald* called the "moral center of Texas") wrote a series of historical articles in the *Texas Baptist and Herald* in which he recounted the deeds of the heroes of the Texas Revolution and the triumphs of the missionaries to Texas. "Texas has the material for a grander epic than Homer's immortal Iliad, or the more beautiful epic of the Aeneid of Virgil," he wrote. "In this glorious history Baptist men and women have acted a glorious part, as pathfinders and foundation builders." Burleson himself claimed no small part in that epic. "General Houston was awakened and converted under my preaching, and I buried him a Baptist," he reported. "I taught his children at Independence, and have often talked the hours away, until after midnight, about the past and the present and the future."[30]

Burleson saw his principal role as a historian rather than as participant in the epic. As pastoral confidant to important figures in the history of Texas he felt himself uniquely qualified to tell the story. Not only did he know Sam Houston well, but his relationship with Susannah Dickinson, a survivor of the battle of the Alamo, entitled him to write about that conflict with confidence: "In the providence of God; the heroine of the Alamo was also converted under my preaching, and I baptized her, and have spent many hours with her in religious instruction, during which the whole scenes of the Alamo and 1836 were detailed and carefully noted."[31]

Burleson's historical essays blended biblical, classical, and southern themes. Stephen F. Austin, "the father and founder of Texas," was particularly selected for his work. "His spotless purity, his chivalrous sense of honor, his patient toils, his unselfish devotion to Texas and to his plighted honor to Mexico," Burleson wrote, "all show that God especially fitted him for his great work." However, his credentials not withstanding, Austin could not finish the work alone. There was one even greater. "The student of Texas history must recognize the fact that Gen. Sam Houston was the savior of Texas," Burleson insisted. "He was a God-sent and a divinely qualified man." Still, Burleson did not want to leave the impression that these two heroes were altogether unlike their contemporaries. "We must also remember that Austin and Houston were only Titans among Titans . . . *primi inter pares* among a race of heroes." he wrote. "Not to recognize these great facts is to do injustice to Austin and Houston and the wisdom and goodness of God in sending a race of heroes to lay deep and broad the foundation of the grandest State between the oceans."

Burleson anticipated a large and eager audience for his essays ("all the world will fire to know all about the men, whose blood, tears, and heroism rescued this paradise . . . from Mexican misrule and the Indian's scalping knife"), but he recognized that others might tell the story differently. He would not question their veracity because "there are two sides to a board . . . and witnesses immaculately honest may see and relate the same thing from different standpoints, and may seem contradictory." There was also an important precedent for these apparent contradictions in the accounts of participant/chroniclers. "This is manifest among the Holy Evangelists themselves," he reminded his readers.

In later years the story of the egging of the prohibition speakers would occasionally appear in histories, subject to the same fluidity of detail about which Burleson cautioned. In 1907, B.F. Riley published his *History of the Baptists of Texas*, in which the event served to illustrate the evangelistic courage and effectiveness of B.H. Carroll, who had been provoked to go to San Antonio to speak following the incident. In B.F. Riley's retelling of the incident, which seems to be drawn loosely from contemporary accounts and from the Acts of the Apostles, the mayor of San Antonio slaps the face of a Methodist minister who is trying to give a prohibition speech. Carroll, with "the courage of the lion," was infuriated by this overt (and inveterate) assault on the minister's honor. He "felt toward San Antonio somewhat as Paul felt toward the Roman capital," and immediately resolved to take the prohibition message there.[32]

Another contribution to the sacred history of Texas was *Texas Garlands*, a volume of poems published by Martha Whitten in 1886. Whitten had a wide readership in Texas, particularly after her poem "The Drunkard's Wife" was issued as a campaign pamphlet in 1887. The book published the year before contained a number of religious and historical poems, including a longer one addressed to "The Old Alamo." In it Whitten honors the heroic dead of the Alamo, and also makes clear who is to be excluded from the epic:

> One look upon these battered, ruined walls,
> What visions of the past the scene recalls!
> Not of the kneeling Priest or gentle Nun
> Who worshiped here when first thy life begun;
> Not of the dusky hordes who gathered here betime
> To worship at the matin hour, or vesper chime —
> Ah, no, 'tis not for these and these alone
> That Texans honor now this hulk of stone —
> Within these walls (for aye the Texan's pride)
> A mere handful of men Santa Anna's hosts defied.[33]

For these evangelicals, the new history of Texas would begin with the revolution, the immigration of white Southerners, and the establishment of southern Protestantism.[34]

The prohibition amendment to the state constitution was seen by its advocates as the next phase of this history. "According to President Burleson, 'Texas' means 'Paradise,'" editor Hayden of the *Texas Baptist and Herald* reminded his readers. "Let us make it all that Dr. Burleson claims for it by voting whisky out of it." And he had very clear ideas as to what sort of paradise prohibition would bring. "Give us prohibition in Texas," he declared, "and a half million of the best people in the older States will make our prairies blossom next year, and the prices of lands will double in less than five years."[35]

The 1887 campaign disrupted Texas politics and divided Texans along ethnic and religious lines. At issue in the minds of the prohibition champions was not simply the continuation or prohibition of the sale and manufacture of alcoholic beverages. Rather, these southern evangelicals believed that at stake was the future of the society in which they lived. They hoped to fashion a social order which would reflect the best elements of white southern culture. The prohibitionists envisioned, and positioned, themselves both as reformers and as legitimate descendants of the Old South and of the Texas Revolution. They did not advocate a return to a mythical antebellum South. Their reformed society would be capitalistic, modern, and governed by a comprehensive system of law, even if it would not be egalitarian. Nevertheless their understanding of their society was infused with a code of behavior that evoked deep and immediate responses. That code did not simply exist alongside their evangelical theology; it informed their view of themselves, their social and political aspirations, and their sense of their role in the unfolding of God's plan. They also realized the challenges they faced in persuading voters to accept their vision of the future. The amendment advocates received more favorable press in the wake of the egging controversy, but it was not clear that they would have the votes to carry the day of August 4. Honor required not that they win, but that they fight well. As the editor of the *Texas Christian Advocate* proclaimed, "we scarcely hoped to win it; we were mobilizing an army." Once mobilized they could be confident of victory, for this prohibition army would be "made up of the bone and sinew of the land; the best and bravest blood of the country runs in its veins." Moreover, the prohibitionists were able to mold themselves in the images of their own mythical creation: We "made a gallant fight," the *Texas Christian Advocate* proclaimed at the end of the campaign, "the finest the State ever saw since Travis defended the Alamo." Because it was an honorable cause, prohibition was the legitimate heir to the heroes of the Texas Revolution. Even those southern evangelicals whose Texas heritage did not reach back fifty years to those glorious days (Rev. Sutherland and Rev. Burleson were exceptional in that regard) could understand the sentiment. If the prohibitionists did not carry the day on August 4, they, like those who died at the Alamo, would face an honorable defeat. In that there would be no disgrace, as S.A. Hayden reminded the readers of the *Texas Baptist and Heritage*, because "no cause with martyrs ever fails." The Rev. Sutherland did not pay the ultimate price levied on the warriors of '36 or the prohibitionist Roderick Gambrell, but the eggs that splattered him in the 1887 battle of the Alamo were as surely badges of honor as were the wounds of those fallen heroes.[36]

Chapter 5

"Who Brought This New Idea into Texas, Anyhow?"[1]

Texans Reject Prohibition

On the morning of August 4, 1887, the majority of retail businesses (the saloons most conspicuously) remained closed as the polls opened around the state. Texans began voting early, walking or riding alone or in groups. In some cases they arrived at the polls in wagons provided by competing sides in the struggle, the antis in particular having arranged for hired conveyances. There was considerable electioneering at the polling places. Preprinted ballots were passed out by both sides with "for prohibition" or "against prohibition" marked in advance, a courtesy to voters that could shade easily to fraud. At Caldwell prohibitionists reportedly handed out to black voters ballots printed on circular pieces of paper, a practice often adopted by Republicans to assist freedmen who could not read. Like in previous elections, these were marked "Republican Ticket" prominently at the top, despite the fact that no candidates were standing for election that day. The relevant portion of the ballot was the "for prohibition" printed in smaller characters lower on the ballot. At El Paso the antis were accused of bringing in voters from Mexico and conveying them from precinct to precinct to cast multiple ballots. Even the staunchly anti-prohibitionist Galveston *Daily News* expressed outrage. "Few if any of the Mexicans were paid money for their votes," the editor stormed. "They were filled up with beer." A more subtle enticement was provided by the women of the WCTU, who set up booths in most of the cities to provide food, iced tea, and lemonade. Even in notoriously anti-prohibitionist San Antonio the WCTU set up booths early in the day, only to abandon the effort in the afternoon after suffering "jeers and insults" from the gathered citizens. Their efforts in other cities elicited a more favorable response, although at Galveston one of the ladies participating was uncertain of the picnic's effectiveness. "I think some of those men were just too hateful for anything to come into our booth and eat lunch, and then go and vote against prohibition," she complained. "Plenty of them did it, and they ought to be ashamed of themselves."[2]

The concern expressed about potential fraudulent voting had prompted State Attorney General Jim Hogg to issue a ruling on voter qualification. He ruled that residency in the state for at least a year was required, but that the requirement for residency in a particular county, as had often been the practice in prior elections, was not lawful. His office was kept busy responding to questions from local judges and wiring responses throughout the day. Despite the attempt to centralize and standardize requirements for eligibility, precinct election judges exercised considerable discretion in determining who was qualified to vote and the degree to which balloting was done secretly. At the local level the attorney general's rulings were not always followed.[3]

Nowhere was the balloting more closely watched or the issue more hotly contested than at Waco. Both the prohibitionists and the anti-prohibitionists had their headquarters in that city. The night before the vote both sides had staged grand rallies. The next morning the polling places around the city—mostly schools, post offices, or retail establishments—were festooned with banners. Brass bands played on the streets throughout the day. At least one group of prohibitionists gathered early and marched in parade to the polls to vote. There was little evidence of the fraudulent voting that was rumored in other cities. A new system of switching out ballot boxes hourly and keeping a running tally through the day allowed for returns to be announced minutes after the polls closed. The results stunned the prohibitionists: Waco had voted against the amendment. Still they had cause for hope. The majority against the amendment in the town had been a mere twenty-nine votes.[4]

At the headquarters of each side, officials reviewed and announced returns from around the state as soon as results were wired in. At the anti headquarters Chairman George Clark stood and read the dispatches as county after county turned in a majority against the amendment. At the prohibition headquarters, supporters set up a magic lantern to project the returns on the wall of the building. As the crowd became more bored and dejected, pictures replaced the discouraging numbers. Around the city bonfires blazed as the results became more generally known. A parade spontaneously formed and marched to the anti headquarters to hear speeches from Clark and others. The next day the celebration continued with more fires, speeches, and parades, as further returns solidified the anti majority. By the evening of the fifth, with seventy-seven counties still unaccounted for, the antis were claiming a majority of seventy-five thousand votes.[5]

Similar celebrations occurred throughout the state. At San Antonio, where the Galveston *Daily News* had reported that "contrary to expectation, the election passed off without a single fight," black anti-prohibitionists circulated leaflets declaring that the funeral of Bishop Turner would be celebrated in the evening. The city marshal broke up the procession just as it was forming on Military Plaza. At Dallas, in the midst of the celebration, a man rode his horse through the doors and up to the bar of the Glen Lea Saloon. Without dismounting he called for a drink, was served, and rode back into the street. At Corsicana "anti-prohibition ladies" hosted a banquet attended by Congressman Roger Mills. Diners called for fourteen toasts in the course of the evening, honoring the congressman; "'the Ladies, God bless 'em'; the bible; the Young Democracy of Texas; the Law; Jefferson Davis; and the farmers of the state," among other worthies. At Burnet victorious antis formed a torchlight procession that marched throughout the town, and then proceeded west to the top of Post mountain where they set off a hundred charges of dynamite to punctuate the victory. A correspondent at the scene was able to report that "no disturbance of any kind occurred either during the celebration by the antis or during the election," probably leaving readers to wonder exactly what might constitute a disturbance.[6]

The prohibitionists had less cause for celebration. Final returns gave them fewer than 130,000 votes out of nearly 350,000 cast. Thirty-two counties out of 181 returned majorities for the amendment. Of all the cities, only Fort Worth voted with the prohibitionists. San Antonio rejected the amendment by a vote of 4,861 to 507. In heavily German New Braunfels, 409 votes were cast, every single one against the amendment. At Waco, the state executive committee met in a closed session at the First Baptist Church on August 16 to wrap up business and disband. Not even sympathetic reporters were allowed in the building, one less sympathetic told that "it was more of a family gathering than anything else," and that members might report to the press at a later time. For the prohibitionists the time had come to take stock of the returns, discover what went wrong, and plan for the future.[7]

Not all were willing to accept defeat graciously. Although there is no evidence that fraud was widespread, or that it was by any means prevalent enough to have had any bearing on the final outcome of the vote, some prohibitionists questioned whether they had really lost the fight fairly. "It is astounding how the majority against Prohibition in Texas continues increasing since the vote was taken," remarked a correspondent to the *Union Signal*. "If this continues at the rate it is now going on, the majority will soon exceed the voting population of the state." This concern was not entirely unjustified. Two counties, Navarro and Rusk, counted more votes in 1887 than voting-age males in the 1890 census.[8]

The *Texas Christian Advocate* presented a table of voters, including "Colored votes," "German votes," "Naturalized votes," "Saloon votes," and "Fraudulent votes"; and concluded that these five groups made up the greater part of the anti vote. In a letter to the *New York Voice*, Sen. John Reagan reported that "prohibition was defeated by the votes of the negroes, Germans and Mexicans." He also concluded, "a majority of the native Americans and of the Democrats of Texas have voted for prohibition." The prohibitionist editors of the Dallas *Daily Herald* proclaimed that "two-thirds to three-fourths of the Democrats of Texas are for this reform movement" and that "without the colored and foreign vote yesterday, prohibition would today have 60,000 majority." The *Union Signal* reported that "the large German vote counted for free beer, and the considerable Jewish family were an 'anti' unit" and that "Mexico and Mexicans swore and fought for the saloon."[9]

The prohibitionists' analysis of the returns was obviously colored by the bitterness of defeat and based on the impressions of reporters who were less than objective. They were looking for scapegoats as much as explanations for the rejection by Texans of the prohibition amendment. A closer examination of the returns can provide more accurate information. A quantitative analysis of the vote may not explain why Texans rejected prohibition, but it can go a long way toward identifying which Texans opposed the amendment.[10]

Voter turnout was extraordinarily high in the amendment election. In the previous year an estimated 66% of eligible voters had turned out for the general election. The prohibition amendment drew approximately 72% of eligible voters, although there were no political offices at stake. The following table provides information about those Texans who voted on the amendment:

Table 5.1

Estimated Voter Participation in the 1887 Prohibition Amendment Vote[11]

	Total Eligible	% of Eligible	Number Voted	Participation	% of Vote Cast
Native White Males	323,436	67.0%	254,865	78.8%	73.1%
Foreign-Born White Males	65,957	13.7%	22,596	34.3%	6.5%
African American Males	93,194	19.3%	71,335	76.5%	20.4%
Totals	482,587	100%	348,796	72.3%	100%

One significant result in these findings is the extraordinarily high level of participation among African American voters. These results are consistent with the recriminations of prohibitionists in the days following the vote. Black voters could not be blamed for having contributed to the defeat of the amendment unless they had gone to the polls in significant numbers.[12]

But did race or nativity have any bearing on support for the amendment at the polls? Before August 4, both sides had assiduously courted African Americans, organizing "colored" anti and prohibitionists clubs, employing black orators (who frequently shared a stage with their white counterparts) and publicizing the admonitions and predictions of prominent black Texans. Certainly the prohibitionists had expressed the greater trepidation about the impact of the black vote on the outcome, but they had not given up hope on the eve of the balloting. Although African Americans accounted for a fifth of the electorate, if they turned out in high numbers and voted as a block, they could have had a considerable impact on the final tally. Foreign-born voters were a smaller group, but prohibitionists had viewed them all along as a threat to the cause. How justified were the prohibitionists in blaming black and foreign-born voters for the defeat of the amendment? The following tables present a calculated estimate of the vote for prohibition, taking into account the previous calculations on voter turnout:

Table 5.2

Estimated Vote on Prohibition in 1887: Votes Cast by Race and Nativity[13]

	For Prohibition	Against Prohibition	Total Vote
Native White Males	115,008	139,857	254,865
Foreign-Born White Males	1,970	20,626	22,596
African American Males	11,857	59,478	71,335
Totals	128,835	219,961	348,796

Table 5.3

Estimated Vote for Prohibition in 1887: Percentages by Race and Nativity

	Percent of Total Vote	Percent for Prohibition	Percent of Prohibition Vote	Percent of Anti Vote
Native White	73.1%	45.1%	89.3%	63.6%
Foreign-Born White	6.5%	8.7%	1.5%	9.4%
African American	20.4%	16.6%	9.2%	27.0%
Totals	100%	36.9%	100%	100%

It is evident from the tables that African Americans and foreign-born voters overwhelmingly opposed the prohibition amendment. But it is also important to note that the majority of native white males also voted against prohibition, and that the majority of votes against the amendment were cast by native whites.

Where then did support for the amendment arise? First of all, prohibition was a product of the white southern evangelical churches. Baptist and Methodist ministers and members made up the great part of the prohibition leadership, and by all accounts support for the amendment in local congregations was more than sufficient to foster expectations of the movement's success. But prohibitionists, while not denying their denominational roots, worked hard to present themselves as secular reformers, and they did this by utilizing culturally southern tropes to establish credibility with potential voters. To the degree they succeeded, there should be evidence of support for the amendment among those Texans with the closest ties to white southern culture.

A simple way to do this would be to examine the support for prohibition in that portion of the population born outside of Texas but in other states of the former Confederacy, and contrast that with support among native Texans. A bivariate correlation produces striking results. There is a strong positive correlation ($r^2 = .722$) between the vote for prohibition and the percentage of Texans born in other southern states in county-level aggregate data. A moderate negative correlation ($r^2 = -.447$) exists between the prohibition vote and the percentage of native Texans in the same population. But these figures obscure other important elements. Among the native Texans were ethnic Germans and Mexicans who were much less likely than the general population to support prohibition. Moreover, because a considerable portion of the African American migration to Texas had occurred in the years prior to and during the Civil War, black Texans were more likely than their white counterparts to be counted as natives of the state. A more useful contrast would be between native white Texans and white Texans born in other southern states.

This can be accomplished by a regression of county-level voter returns for the state, calculated with four independent variables: percent native Texan, percent born in other southern states, percent foreign-born voters, and percent African American voters. Because of the low turnout among foreign-born voters, the inclusion of that variable provides a control both for the foreign-born vote and for the increased incidence of ethnic German and Mexicans among native-born Texans. The inclusion of African American voters provides a control for the increased incidence of African Americans among the native-born. In calculating partial correlations the addition of an independent variable for African Americans does not exclude them from the Texas-born and southern-born populations, because each black voter is also a member of one of those two groups. The effect of the variable is to distribute evenly the impact of the black vote in the two groups.

Controlling for the other independent variables yields partial correlation coefficients of -.218 for native-Texan voters and +.195 for southern-born voters who are not native Texans. After subtracting the black vote, it is reasonable to conclude that only 31.7% of Texas-born white voters favored prohibition. This figure would be lower if it included all of the ethnic German and Mexican native-born Texans, but overcompensating for foreign-born voters allows a more useful comparison of two critical groups of Texans: white Southerners who migrated to Texas on the one hand and white Texans whose parents or grandparents had migrated to Texas from the other southern states a few decades earlier. The results are striking. Texas-born white voters overwhelmingly opposed prohibition in the 1887 campaign. In contrast, 57.4% of all native white Southerners not born in Texas voted for prohibition. No other group of Texans voted a majority in favor of the measure.[14]

The correlation between support for prohibition and southern nativity can be viewed geographically. The following maps illustrate the county-level correlation between the two groups:[15]

Figure 5.1

Vote for the Prohibition Amendment, 1887

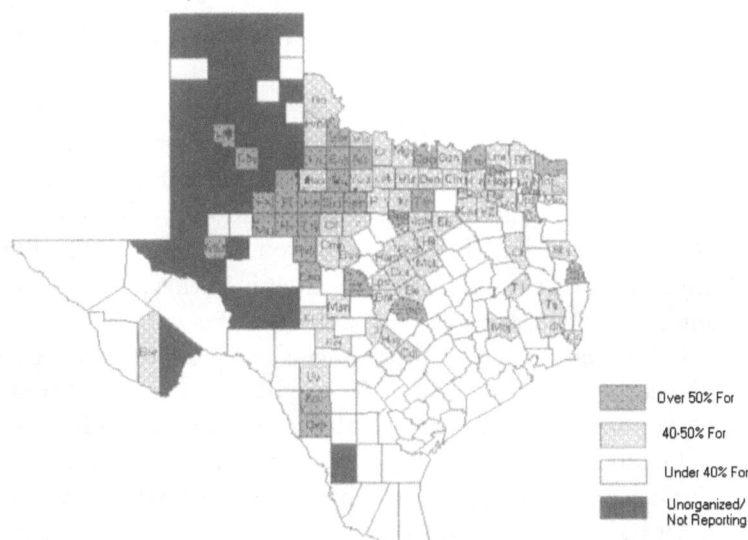

Figure 5.2
Percent Born in Other Southern States, 1880

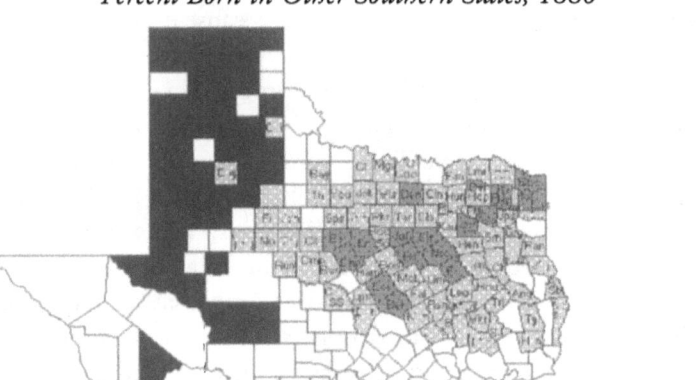

As the maps demonstrate, prohibitionists and Southerners were concentrated in north-central and northeast Texas. Moving toward the Gulf coastal plains, support for prohibition drops off while southern nativity remains concentrated. These counties had a higher proportion of African Americans in the population. If African Americans could be excluded at the county level, then the two maps would demonstrate an even closer correlation. The counties with the highest proportion of southern-born whites had the highest returns for prohibition.[16]

What could explain the striking difference between support for prohibition among native whites born in Texas and those born in other southern states? For the sake of caution, a part of the difference should be ascribed to the inclusion of Tejanos and German Texans in the native Texan population, despite the efforts to adjust for those two groups in the analysis. But there would still be a significant difference in the voting behavior of Anglo voters unaccounted for. There were cultural differences between the native white southern Texans and the native Texan Anglos that led one group to support prohibition and the other to reject it. The southern whites came from states with a more homogenous culture: close ties to the Old South, established evangelical churches, and what they perceived as a clear racial line uncomplicated by issues of ethnicity. Texan Anglos had lived with more complexity: an independent Texas history predating the Confederacy, evangelical churches struggling on a frontier and competing with an established Catholic church, and Tejano and German neighbors (or at least fellow Texans) who had a valid claim of precedence and whose own cultures had shaped the broader Texan culture since before statehood.[17]

The same statistical methodology used to determine voting patterns by race and nativity can be applied to address another issue that arose in the course of the prohibition campaign. Despite the efforts of many political leaders, the issue of prohibition became entwined with party politics. Anti-prohibitionists in particular, accused their opponents of political heresy. Prohibition, they insisted, was not compatible with the principles and doctrines of the party of Jefferson. The "True Blues" sought to discredit the reformers by accusing them of willfully threatening the hegemony of the Democratic Party in Texas and across the South. Prohibitionists were usually more cautious about bringing up issues of party loyalty, because a division existed among their ranks on these issues. Some emphasized their fealty to the Democratic Party; others joined ranks with the partisan Prohibitionists. Nevertheless, prohibitionists were also willing to resort to partisan attack when it suited their purposes. They pointed out, correctly, that African Americans and ethnic Germans were generally opposed to prohibition and generally loyal to the Republican Party. It would be useful to determine if these arguments were reflected in the electorate.[18]

Unfortunately, the prohibition vote did not coincide with a general election for statewide offices. Indeed, Democratic officeholders had set the date of the election at a time when no offices were to be filled with the intent of avoiding a partisan fight on the issue. Nevertheless, it is possible to examine the previous year's election results in the gubernatorial race to see if there exists any link between party affiliation and support for prohibition.

In 1886 Texans had gone to the polls and elected Democrat Lawrence "Sul" Ross over Republican candidate A.M. Cochran and Prohibitionist Eben Dohoney. The vote was not close: Ross received 223,654 or 72.6% of the 308,151 votes tabulated. Cochran ran a distant second with 21.7%, and Dohoney received 6.4% of the vote. Cochran fared well with black voters, and made a respectable showing in the Hill Country counties with large German populations. Dohoney was probably not even on the ballot in many counties, and his overall support was not significant enough to correlate with the following year's vote in any useful way.

An analysis of the vote suggest that Texas Republicans overwhelmingly rejected prohibition, with fewer than a quarter of voters casting ballots for the Republican gubernatorial candidate in 1886 voting in favor of prohibition in 1887. Given the ethnic makeup of the party in the state, this is not particularly surprising. The results are less clear concerning the Democratic vote. There is, at first glance, a weak correlation between Democratic voters in 1886 and support for prohibition in 1887, but that correlation disappears when the Republican vote is controlled at the county level. Statistically speaking, it is safe to conclude only that Texas Republicans opposed prohibition, and that Texas Democrats were divided on the issue.[19]

Of course prohibitionist leaders and editors who decried the impact of the black and foreign vote were not unaware that a significant portion of native white voters, including many Democrats, had opposed the amendment. Many of them had become accomplished statisticians in the course of the campaign, using census data and congressional reports to bolster their arguments about the positive economic and social results of prohibition. The fact that anti-prohibitionist leaders were also partisan Democrats could be overlooked if their constituents had voted for the amendment, but prohibitionists would have known that such an overwhelming defeat could only have resulted from the rejection of the amendment by a great number of southern Democrats.

Prohibitionists who addressed the issue of the defection of southern Democrats found a cause in an event that had occurred nine days before the votes were cast. On July 26, anti-prohibitionists had held their largest rally of the campaign at Fort Worth, with estimates of as many as fifty thousand in attendance. On the podium had been five Democratic congressmen, the state attorney general, the father of the governor, and State Treasurer and former Governor F.R. Lubbock. Lubbock produced and read to the crowd a letter addressed to him from former Confederate President Jefferson Davis, for whom he had served as aide-de-camp and with whom he had been captured at the end of the war. Writing from his home in Beauvoir, Mississippi, Davis apologized for injecting his opinions into Texas politics, but declared that the threat to individual liberty posed by prohibition required him to ask Texans to reject the amendment as inimical to Democratic principles.[20]

The anti-prohibitionists had quickly exploited the letter to attack the Democratic credentials of the prohibitionists. Quotations from the letter appeared in editorials in a number of anti-prohibitionist papers. Prohibitionists, on the other hand, had a difficult time responding. S.A. Hayden, of the *Texas Baptist and Herald*, tried to turn it to the advantage of the reformers. "The trumped up letter of Jefferson Davis read at the Fort Worth whisky rally is proving a boomerang in the hands of the antis," he wrote. "The colored people in South Texas cannot understand how the prohibition movement is intended to bring them into slavery when the ex-President of the Confederacy opposes its adoption." But most prohibitionists, realizing the potential damage to their movement the letter represented, expressed only confusion and dismay. Senator John Reagan, who had served as Davis' postmaster general, wrote to the former Confederate leader a letter that was reprinted widely. "I write not to complain, but to express my surprise and sorrow on account of the letter you wrote to our good friend, Governor Lubbock," Reagan wrote. "Texas has never been so profoundly stirred up on a question before within my memory." He explained to Davis that the prohibitionists had hoped to be able to prevail, even "against the combined influence and efforts of the manufacturers of whisky and beer, the Liquor Dealers' Association of St. Louis, Chicago, Louisville, Cincinnati, New York, Philadelphia and elsewhere, and against the use of the vast sums of money they have sent to Texas to employ and pay speakers, suborn the newspapers and corrupt the ballot and debauch our people." But now they were opposed by the "talismanic power of your great name," and feared that it would mean the defeat of the amendment.[21]

After the vote, prohibitionists listed the Davis letter as one of the causes of the amendment's defeat. Like Reagan, critics felt betrayed by his opposition to prohibition, but few resorted to attacks on the former Confederate leader. An exception was a set of brief reprints from southern newspapers that appeared in the *Texas Christian Advocate*. The *Raleigh* (North Carolina) *Advocate*'s editor expressed the opinion that Davis was senile; the *Holston Methodist* of Knoxville, Tennessee declared that Davis' letter was "enough to mantle the fair Southern cheek with shame." The *Alabama Advocate* of Birmingham was among the harshest: "The people of the South among whom Mr. Davis lives, and thousands of men who followed him through the war, have been struggling against this giant evil for years, and now, just on the eve of victory, Mr. Davis sells out to the whisky devil," the editor wrote. "It were better for Mr. Davis, and better for the South, if he had rotted in the dungeons of Fortress Monroe than to have been the instrument of enslaving the people of Texas for years to come." The indictment was clear. By opposing prohibition in Texas, Jefferson Davis had become a traitor to the South. The prohibitionists, in contrast, were the authentic and loyal Southerners.[22]

Many observers and partisans felt that the issue of prohibition would fade from Texas politics now that the voters had spoken so decisively on the matter. "The silver-tongued orator can now take a rest," one editor wished. "So can a patient and long afflicted public." Before a jubilant anti-prohibition crowd at Waco, former Senator Richard Coke declared that the youngest boy present would not live to see the issue revived in the state. A few of the staunchest anti-prohibition Democrats hoped to insert a plank in the state party's 1888 platform repudiating prohibition altogether, but a compromise was reached in which the results of the election were accepted without comment. The *Texas Christian Advocate* explained to readers that as a religious paper it must now turn its attention to other sectarian matters, notwithstanding the fact that many had begun subscribing in the previous months just to follow the news of the prohibition campaign. The State Prohibition Executive Committee under the leadership of the Rev. Dr. B.H. Carroll released an "Address to the Prohibitionists of Texas" in which they acknowledged the judgment of the state's voters, and recommended that the issue not be revived in the next legislature.[23]

Many prohibitionists were not so ready to abandon the cause. The Rev. Atticus Haygood, who had left his native Georgia to campaign in Texas during the summer, wrote to the editor of the *Wesleyan Advocate*, "these Texans if they fail today, will begin tomorrow to get ready for another fight." Major John Richardson declared in the *Texas Christian Advocate*, "the victory is just ahead. Let us close up our ranks, march on and gain it." Echoing these martial strains a correspondent to the *Union Signal* wrote, "the spirit that remembered Bunker Hill before Yorktown will . . . march on short rations and barefoot over cactus-plants, until Texas shall celebrate the Yorktown of the traffic." The *Texas Christian Advocate* predicted, "prohibition is not buried, and it will reign in Texas before six years more have passed."[24]

Although the effort to restrict access to liquor by local option would continue in Texas and throughout the South in the years to follow, it would be nearly a quarter of a century before Texans would vote again on the issue of statewide prohibition. By 1911, when another prohibition amendment would appear on the ballot, the political and social landscape that circumscribed the movement would lead prohibitionists to adopt new strategies in the struggle. But in 1887 they saw their best chances for success in a movement that emphasized conservatism, paternalism, and regionalism. Party politics, the central role of the clergy, and the place of women in the reform movement were downplayed in an effort to persuade male Texans to vote for the amendment.

Jenny Bland Beauchamp, president of the Texas WCTU, blasted the southern strategy of the male prohibitionists. "The conduct of the late campaign was radically wrong," she wrote in an article entitled "The Lesson of the Defeat" and published in the *Texas Baptist and Herald*. "The most important Christian principles were surrendered," she charged. "The most useful agencies were neglected." The prohibitionist leadership adopted this timid strategy, she added with unrestrained irony, "out of respect to the prejudices of the anti leaders." Because the anti-prohibitionists criticized the involvement of "the fanatical preachers," prohibitionists requested that ministers "take a back seat" in the campaign. But "the anti leaders were wise," she argued, and "knew the power of the Christian ministry." The antis were able to force the prohibitionists to refuse the assistance of "outside help" by crying "Yankee influence!" and "Short-haired women!" According to Beauchamp, prohibitionists would have profited from the assistance of such "practiced warriors" as "Bain, Willard, Green, Clay, Smith, Lathrop and others." And of course in rejecting the assistance of women, Beauchamp believed that the prohibitionists had made the gravest error. When "the anti leaders tried to drive her out of the field by innuendoes of immodest women and female suffrage," the male prohibitionists beat a coward's retreat. They "turned pale; their knees smote together; they said 'We must not let the women in; it is too unpopular.'" Lest any of her male prohibitionist counterparts fail to comprehend her attack on their division of labor in the movement, she continued. "The W.C.T.U. might have been a great power in this struggle," she wrote. "Our Prohibition brothers, as true subordinates, tried to carry out the policy of our leaders."[25]

Beauchamp's criticism would have been particularly stinging to the male prohibitionists. She assailed their courage and their presumption of leadership, all the while reminding them that they had been defeated. To men reared in a southern patriarchy, this would have cut deeply. But Beauchamp was making the point that it was precisely this southern patriarchy, with its rejection of a partnership with women and "outsiders," and its ambivalence toward evangelical activism, despite the fact that so many of them were themselves clerics, that had caused the defeat of the amendment. The men "had not been educated out of narrow prejudices. They were too self-sufficient to profit by counsel." The women, she pointed out, could have done better. It was an affront to the honor of the male prohibitionists, but as men of honor they were bound to ignore her, and none responded in print to her critique.[26]

It is by no means certain that the 1887 prohibition campaign would have been more successful had the men leading the fight followed Beauchamp's advice. The antis had been the first to attack the participation of clergymen, women, and outsiders in the campaign. The prohibitionist reacted by downplaying the role of these groups because the criticism resonated so forcefully in both camps. Yet Beauchamp had correctly characterized the prohibitionist strategy. In an effort to define prohibition as a native southern reform, they had rejected their most experienced allies. It had been necessary to do so to persuade southern white males to vote for the amendment. Their vote was divided and there were not enough of them, and there were too many of everyone else; however it was precisely these southern white males who had provided the greatest support for prohibition.

Prohibition Rally, Main Square, Nacogdoches, Texas, early twentieth century.

Courtesy of the Center for American History, UT Austin, CH Number 04390

Coda

From a Regional to a National Reform

By 1903 the plazas of San Antonio had long been the setting of public activity. Unlike the rest of the narrow, twisted streets, they were spacious and broad enough to accommodate the political rallies and popular celebrations that occurred so frequently in the city. Parades crossed or circled the plazas in observation of at least five different public holidays, including two specifically Texan; and much of the rest of the year the plazas hosted fiestas, holy days, or Sängerfeste. Even on the more ordinary days, they bustled with shoppers, merchants, and travelers. A visitor was likely to overhear conversations in four languages, and for pocket change could acquire a bottle of ointment guaranteed to cure catarrh or consumption, a pint of whisky, or a promise of salvation.

Alamo Plaza in particular was a popular site for preachers, vendors, and exhorters of every stripe. The speaker was guaranteed a large crowd, and had as a backdrop the most sacred shrine to Texas Independence. In the early, still sunny evening of Friday, August 7, those selling raspas would have been most popular if there were any ice to be shaved, but a fairly substantial crowd had gathered at the north end of the plaza at the Houston Street corner in front of the Maverick Bank. There the Rev. J.K. Wooten, who was described in the next day's *Daily Express* as a "professional temperance and Prohibition preacher," en route from Georgetown to a prohibition rally in Nacogdoches, was admonishing his listeners and displaying "several large canvas hangers, painted with lurid illustrations of the evils of the liquor traffic." Opening with "a fervent text from the second chapter of the Prophet Habakkuk," he shouted, "Woe to them that give drink to their neighbors, and thou that holdest thy bottle to their lips," a favorite passage among speakers who used scripture to castigate saloon keepers.

The police were called, and one Officer Busch "very politely" asked the preacher to move to another spot, as the crowd had delayed three street cars and the sidewalk was so crowded that pedestrians could not pass. When Wooten refused he and at least one of his supporters were arrested. From his cell the Rev. Wooten accused the police of taking him into custody simply for preaching the gospel. "If I hadn't gone for the saloons they wouldn't have interfered," he argued. "It was the saloon people that made them do it." Visiting her husband in jail, Mrs. Wooten questioned the newspaper reporters present: "What kind of a city is this anyway?"[1]

San Antonio was the largest city in Texas in the first decade of the twentieth century, the center of commerce in south Texas. However, despite its prominence in Texas society and history, it was being eclipsed by the booming cities to the north. Its blend of native and immigrant cultures stood in sharp contrast to the more typically southern culture of north Texas. The social life of San Antonio was by no means egalitarian. Racism was as deeply imbedded as anywhere in the state and the legacy of the dispossession and displacement of Tejanos made possible the domination of Anglos and German Texans in public life. Nevertheless, San Antonio typified an older, more diverse culture that contrasted sharply with the enthusiastic boosterism and reformist zeal of many north Texans.[2]

San Antonio's population would continue to increase, but the urban boom in Houston and Dallas would soon eclipse it. Dallas in particular was a demographic upstart, its population growing from 3,000 in 1870 to over 92,000 (compared with San Antonio's 96,000) in 1910. Nearly three hundred miles north of San Antonio where the Texas and Pacific Railroad crossed the western edge of Texas' Blackland Prairie, Dallas was fast becoming an important economic and cultural center for a new generation of entrepreneurs. There was a substantial African American population in the city, but most of the residents were white Southerners. By 1911, the year of the second statewide prohibition vote, Dallas also had become the hub of southern evangelical religion in the state. Southern Methodist University was in the city, and the Baptists had Baylor University at Waco ninety miles to the south and Southwestern Theological Seminary at Fort Worth thirty miles to the west. Dallas was also home to the two largest circulating religious newspapers, the *Baptist Standard* and the Methodists' *Texas Christian Advocate*. Moreover, the Anti-Saloon League, which had begun operating in Texas just a few years earlier, published its state paper, *Home and State*, in Dallas. North Texas had become the stronghold of a regional Anglo-Protestant establishment that would try to assert its hegemony over the entire state in the prohibition campaign.[3]

The prohibitionists had made significant inroads in the years since the 1887 statewide vote, but their success had been geographically limited.

Individual counties, towns, and precincts had the authority to ban alcohol on a local option, and by 1903 most of north Texas was dry. But this partial success was of little value to prohibitionists when bootlegging and access to nearby wet counties made enforced abstinence virtually impossible. Moreover, the ethnic and cultural diversity of central and southern portions of the state continued to be a barrier to local prohibition efforts. "The liquor traffic, entrenched behind the vagrant and mercenary vote in the cities, and behind the foreign-born and the negro vote in Central and South Texas counties," complained one prohibitionist author, "could not be dislodged by a precinct or county vote."[4]

The German Texans, an important element of the "foreign" vote, remained concentrated in ten counties of central Texas. Many were descendants of the German settlers who had been awarded or had purchased portions of land grants from the Republic of Texas in the early 1840s, before most of the North Texas Anglos had moved to the state. In the small towns of the central Texas Hill Country and further south in San Antonio they played an important, often dominant, role in politics and local culture. Nevertheless, because they retained much of German culture, language, and religion (most were Catholic or Lutheran), they were generally viewed as outsiders by the state political and religious leaders to the north.[5]

More significant numerically were the Tejanos, the Texan Hispanics, many of whom were descendants of the earliest settlers in the region. Most lived in the southern third of the state, and their population was increasing annually because of further migration from Mexico. Overwhelmingly Catholic, they appeared to the prohibitionist Anglo-Protestants to be foreign in culture, language, and religion. Most had no interest in supporting prohibition either locally or as a statewide reform.[6]

At the end of the Civil War a third of the population of Texas was African American. That proportion would decrease regularly in successive decades; but in many counties, especially in urban areas and in the eastern half of the state, African Americans made up a sizeable number of potential votes. But the political power of the black electorate had been diminished substantially by the adoption of a poll tax in 1903. As the Democratic Party strengthened its grip on statewide offices, African Americans were less likely to turn out to vote in the face of intimidation and taxation in what had become exercises in ratification of the Democratic Party's candidate selection. Nevertheless, they represented a significant block of potential voters, and could play an important role in the case of a vote on a local option ordinance or a statewide constitutional amendment.

Several factors contributed to the reemergence of prohibition as an important issue in Texas in the first decade of the twentieth century. The national Prohibition Party, which had appeared in the late nineteenth century, had never offered a serious threat to the Democratic Party in the southern states, but it had convinced many in the progressive wing of the party that the "liquor trade" was an important political concern of many voters. The Anti-Saloon League, founded in Ohio in 1895, moved into Texas in 1907 and began to support local option prohibition and to press the legislature to submit another prohibition amendment to the voters. Finally, a progressive reform of the electoral processes in the state made it more likely that a concerted effort on the part of reformers could turn out enough votes to make statewide prohibition a reality.[7]

In 1902 Texas voters ratified the poll tax amendment to the state constitution. The following year in a special session the state legislature passed a law requiring that poll taxes be paid between the first of October and the end of February prior to an election. The statute also made it a crime to pay someone else's poll tax, or to give or loan money to anyone else knowing that the money would be used to pay the poll tax. That same statute, the Terrell Election Law, also required a primary election for all statewide offices, a move that curbed the power of state conventions to select gubernatorial candidates. The political parties were free to institute racial barriers to voting in these primaries since they were not governed by federal election laws. The effect of these reforms was to disfranchise further the poor among two of the groups that had traditionally opposed prohibition—African Americans and Tejanos—while at the same time making statewide campaigns more responsive to the concerns of the remaining Anglo Texan electorate. Responding to pressure from these remaining constituents and to effective lobbying on the part of the Anti-Saloon League, early in 1911 the state legislature approved a constitutional amendment to be submitted to the voters in a general election that summer for the statewide prohibition of "the manufacture, sale, barter, and exchange of intoxicating liquors."[8]

The 1911 prohibition campaign provides an opportunity to contrast the strategies and style of nineteenth- and twentieth-century prohibitionists in Texas. There was significant continuity. The campaign in 1911 was led by evangelical Protestants, African Americans were viewed as significant actors in the outcome of the reform, and women were pushed out—indeed, altogether absent—from the leadership of the movement. The change was in the cultural geography of Texas prohibition. The defensive reliance on southern leaders and the placement of the reform squarely in the context of peculiarly southern culture that had underpinned the campaigns in the 1880s was replaced by a modern, national version of temperance reform. White

Southerners still led the prohibitionist forces, with the southern evangelical churches in particular taking a more visible role than they had since 1882, when they first welcomed Frances Willard into the state. But the unique nature of the campaigns in 1885 and 1887 was the self-conscious anti-clericism that the evangelical leadership incorporated into their own strategies. As Southerners they, even the clerics among them, had been suspicious of an activist clergy. As newcomers to the state they had been sensitive to accusations that they were outsiders, imposing their will on an older society. By 1911 they saw themselves as the leaders of Texas society, the most authentic Texans, and felt no need for caution.

At the turn of the century the majority of white southern Protestants were members of segregated, evangelical, ecclesiastically southern churches. Most of these were Southern Baptists and Southern Methodists (Methodist Episcopal Church, South), each of these bodies numbering over two million members by the second decade of the twentieth century. Members of these two denominations were the most numerous in each of the former Confederate states with the exceptions of Louisiana and Texas. In these two states the number of Roman Catholics was greater than the number of either of the two Protestant denominations, but not greater than the number of Baptists and Methodists combined. Through the nineteenth century, these evangelical churches had progressed from a minority of cultural dissenters into the mainstream of southern culture. These churches, their ministers, colleges and seminaries, newspapers, and denominational institutions formed a regional Protestant Establishment that could wield enormous power in the public life of the southern states.[9]

Texas had been only lately incorporated into that Protestant Establishment. In 1887, when statewide prohibition was first attempted, many of the evangelical Anglo-Protestants had been relative newcomers to the state, migrants from the older southern states. Many of the earlier centers of Texas culture (i.e., San Antonio in south Texas, Galveston on the Gulf coast, and the German towns of central Texas) were mixed communities in which ethnic and cultural diversity was acknowledged, if not sanctioned. Native white Southerners new to Texas had been the greatest supporters of prohibition in 1887, but they had been too few to effect reform. By 1911 they were stronger.

The evangelical churches worked to mobilize the campaign for prohibition that summer. Denominational state conventions adopted resolutions supporting the amendment and gratefully acknowledging the efforts of the Statewide Prohibition Amendment Association and the Texas Anti-Saloon League. The denominational and prohibitionist newspapers reported on each other's efforts to oppose the "liquor interests," and congregations were exhorted on their duty to pay their poll taxes early enough to qualify for the July vote. Methodist Bishop E.D. Mouzon preached a sermon at Travis Park Church in San Antonio on the subject of "The Church and the Saloon," and the text was reprinted in the *Texas Christian Advocate*.[10]

The *Baptist Standard*, the weekly paper of the Texas Baptists, provides a useful window into the mechanics and rhetoric of the 1911 campaign. While the state's daily papers reported extensively on the issue, few of these present such a detailed and unmediated record of the prohibitionists' strategies and goals. The other partisan papers, notably the Methodist *Texas Christian Advocate* and the Anti-Saloon League's *Home and State* also played a role in communicating the issue, but the *Standard* had more resources and readers (claiming 75,000 weekly), making it the most visible journalistic advocate of prohibition in the state.[11]

Nor was the *Baptist Standard* working at odds or in competition with other prohibitionists. Editor James B. Gambrell had been a prominent religious editor and prohibitionist in his native Mississippi before moving to Texas, and maintained close contacts with a number of secular and religious prohibitionist leaders throughout the campaign. Fred Hale, editor of the *Standard*'s "Query Department," credited equally the weeklies of the "Evangelical Christian Denominations" with standing together against the "powerful and far-reaching influence of the daily and weekly press of the State." According to Hale were it not for the religious press, prohibitionists would have had very little opportunity to present their case, as "the editorial department of every great daily political paper in Texas is on the saloon side." Hale's irenic praise for other prohibitionists and his sweeping condemnation of the "saloon side" are characteristic of the campaign generally. As in 1887, other sectarian conflicts were postponed, if not forgotten, in the effort to combat the great evil.[12]

In April, three months before the vote, the Rev. Dr. B.H. Carroll, veteran both of prohibition campaigns and interdenominational feuding, published an article in the *Standard* in which he appealed to all Christians for support. "You are not asked to see in the passage of the amendment some particular advantage to a Methodist, or a Baptist, or a Presbyterian, or an Episcopalian, or a Roman Catholic, but as God's man to settle it in your heart on which side you should align yourself," he wrote. "There is not the slightest reason for you to go into subtle discussion of abstract theories." This cooperative spirit was extended to the secular prohibitionists. The *Standard* reported on prohibition rallies, urging readers to attend. J.H. Gambrell, brother of editor J.B. Gambrell, and himself a former editor of the

Standard, served as the Superintendent of the Texas Anti-Saloon League in 1911. He provided the paper with "Anti-Saloon League Notes" on local option efforts in the state and prohibitionist activities across the nation. James B. Cranfill reemerged as a prohibitionist voice in the paper that he too once had served as editor. Tom Swope, Secretary for the Statewide Prohibition Campaign Committee, offered to provide literature and prohibition song books to the Baptist Young People's Union. "No anti unless he be financially interested, has the temerity to advocate the saloon," Swope proclaimed, "and it will be made more difficult for him when the question of saloon or no saloon is put up to him by one of our bright, sweet-faced girls or promising boys who are doing so great a work in the churches of Texas today."[13]

The secular prohibitionist most frequently provided a platform in the *Standard* was Thomas H. Ball, chairman of the Statewide Prohibition Amendment Association, the organization that had been most influential in pressuring the state legislature to submit the prohibition amendment to the voters. Ball was a highly visible campaigner. He would go on to run unsuccessfully for governor of Texas in 1914, and a story about or by him appeared in the *Standard* almost every week in the months preceding the vote. He solicited money for the campaign, recruited speakers, and distributed literature. On the front page of the issue appearing two days before the balloting he offered a challenge to the ministers of the state regarding the amendment. "No greater service can be performed by Christian ministers than continuous work until the polls close for its success," he argued. "I hope that every minister will spend the remaining days of the campaign actively working and speaking for prohibition in his own county, talking the cause to the people wherever two or three can be gathered together."[14]

With so many organizations working to unite voters behind the amendment campaign, the editors of the *Baptist Standard* felt obliged to sort out the players for their readers. Despite the plethora of organizations, they were "working for the same result, each employing its own methods," Gambrell wrote. "There is absolutely no conflict between them at any point, but complete harmony everywhere."[15]

Not all of the Protestants of Texas cooperated harmoniously in the campaign, however. When the Houston YMCA asked a visiting minister to avoid the issue of prohibition in a talk he was scheduled to give, the *Standard* demanded that the organization drop "Christian" from its name, and declared, "every bar-room man in the country will be for the Y.M.A. in the present fight, and the devil will too." When Texas Governor Oscar B. Colquitt appeared at an anti-prohibition rally in Fort Worth, the *Standard* reported that he had "said on a former occasion that he is an 'unworthy' member of the Methodist church, and we think it ought to go at that." Noting that two "unassociated preachers" had appeared at the same rally, the paper revealed, "one of them got uproariously drunk the next day, as has been abundantly certified. He drank as he prayed." Opposing prohibition could be costly for a minister. Gambrell warned that the cleric who failed to support the amendment "commits ministerial suicide when he goes on the whisky side in the present struggle." Nor was a minister's job the only thing placed in jeopardy were he to be unwilling to preach prohibition. "Men may be preachers, ministers, clergyman, or what not; but let no man who lines up with the bar-rooms profane the holy name of the Christ of God by attaching the word Christian to his name," the *Standard* declared. "That Jesus could have any fellowship with the bar-rooms . . . is a thought too monstrous to indulge."[16]

In contrast to the caution with which earlier prohibitionists had featured their clerical supporters, the secular leadership of the 1911 campaign encouraged ministerial activism. Recalling the language of B.H. Carroll's declaration at the beginning of the 1887 campaign, Statewide Prohibition Amendment Association Chairman Ball announced that "preachers will not take a back seat if our committee can help it." He expected them to "preach prohibition, talk prohibition, and work for prohibition until the polls close." It appears that many did precisely that. The Rev. E.P. West of Denison recalled that it was his "happy privilege to take a heavy part in the fight against the saloon" and that his church "was headquarters for prohibition and the meeting place of a number of great mass meetings." Pastor George Truett of the First Baptist Church of Dallas reported that even were his father running for public office, nothing could induce him to get involved in a "political partisan contest." Nevertheless, concerning the prohibition vote, he declared, "I would no more hold my peace than I would walk into the fire." The Rev. J.T. McNew of West, Texas, expressed a similar lack of misgivings about his clerical involvement. "It's dangerous for a pastor to dabble in such things," he cautioned. "We ought to quit the dabbling business and wade right in."[17]

The *Standard* seconded a suggestion of George Carroll that a collection should be taken in every church in Texas to support the prohibition campaign. When the paper later proposed that churches "cut their pastors loose for one month preceding July 22nd, and send them out as Prohibition Evangelists," the response was enthusiastic. Query Department editor Hale hoped that a "Prohibition Revival Meeting" would be held in every precinct in the state. The voters would "listen to a minister of Christ as he presents the God side of this issue," he predicted, "and as a result of a series of meetings, a sufficient number will be induced to join our ranks to make our cause succeed." Two weeks before the vote editor Gambrell admonished that the five thousand ministers in the state "ought to go in all over from now on." Certainly not every precinct was covered, nor was every minister released to campaign full-time. However, some were. The First Baptist Church of Dallas released the Rev. Truett for three weeks and resolved to defray any expense he might incur in the crusade. The Gaston Avenue Church in the same city sent Pastor Crouch "into the field to help beat down the saloons, the worst enemies to God and His churches." In any case, it is likely that most of the Baptist preachers and many other evangelical clerics heeded the *Standard's* call that "til the sun goes down on July 22 every pulpit in Texas should blaze with moral indignation against the unholy and shameful union of saloon and State."[18]

In defending clerical involvement in the campaign, the *Standard* revived the position of earlier Texas prohibitionists. Because the campaign did not involve political office or partisan loyalties, it was a legitimate arena for ministers. Since the Rev. Truett's father was not running for office, the son could stump for the cause. Editor Gambrell reminded his readers that the Anti-Saloon League was "not a political or factional organization, but represent[ed] all of the evangelical denominations in the war on the saloons." He suggested that pastors should welcome League representatives into their churches and offer them their pulpits in the weeks prior to the vote.[19]

The 1911 prohibitionists did more than simply assert the right of clergy to involve themselves in the campaign. The clergy had a duty to do so. The *Standard* reminded them that it "behooves every preacher in the land to sound out the right note." Moral leadership was required if the government was to function properly. "I have a political speech to make in a Baptist paper," Gambrell declared. "Our government is a government of the people, by the people, and for the people, provided the people themselves run the government and are patriotic enough to be governed by the principles of righteousness." B.H. Carroll weighed in with a challenge to potential critics: "If there be good reasons for opposing a union of church and State," he wrote, "much more for opposing a union of whisky and State."[20]

The attack on the "union of whisky and State" was a recurring theme in the campaign, and reflects the progressive ideology that underpinned much of twentieth-century prohibition rhetoric. Politics was the arena or the struggle between the people and the saloon trust. "The government by saloon will go when the saloon goes, not before," the *Standard* warned. "The only way not to have saloon government is not to have saloons." Bemoaning the "influence of politicians, and the political machinery," Fred Hale wrote that the saloon had purchased "the governor of the State, and his official family, judges, mayors, chiefs of police, sheriffs, United States congressmen and senators, and others who are now or expect to be at the pie counter." Gambrell, in an editorial entitled "Playing Politics in Public Office," predicted that Governor Oscar Colquitt would veto any legislation restricting the hours or licensing of saloons because "he would take care of the liquor interest." But Gambrell went on to predict a popular backlash: "Down in the hearts of the people is the belief that government ought to be carried on in the interest of all people and not some of them." The prohibitionists saw themselves as progressives and as natural allies of the progressive politicians in the state. They attacked the railroads for the practice of giving rebates and reduced rates to preferred customers, such as brewers and delegates to the Statewide Saloon Rally, and reminded the readers of the *Standard* that the defeat of the prohibition amendment would "make any reform along any line tenfold more difficult." The prohibitionists called for, and often received, the support of progressive politicians at the local level. They were particularly hopeful of support in those Texas cities that had been laboratories of municipal reform.[21]

After the 1900 hurricane that devastated Galveston, the survivors adopted the first commission government in the nation's history, and other communities soon followed. Three weeks before the vote, the *Standard* addressed these reformers directly. "The mayor and the commissioners of Dallas, Fort Worth, Houston, Waco, Galveston, Beaumont, San Antonio, Austin, and El Paso, the representatives of what is claimed to be the advanced ideal of municipal purity in this country," exhorted T.N. Jones, "let the people know whether or not this new system is a pretense or a fraud, or a thing of substance which stands for clean politics, the enforcement of the law, and an enlightened civilization in the cities of this commonwealth." The prohibitionists were appealing to progressives affiliated with a national reform culture. In 1911 prohibition was no longer about the future of Texas or the purity of the South. The results of the amendment vote would validate progressive reform on the national level. The regional defense of prohibition had become irrelevant.[22]

Despite their appeal to national issues, the prohibitionists were not optimistic about the support of nationally prominent politicians. With the demise of the Populists and the eclipse of the Prohibition Party by the less partisan Anti-Saloon League, virtually all of the Texas prohibitionists had returned to the Democratic fold. However, at the national level Democrats rarely supported prohibition, and the Republican Party was still too closely associated with Reconstruction to find much support among the Anglo-Protestant voters in the state. Indeed, the *Standard* claimed to have evidence that the most important Republican politicians in the nation had fallen under the spell of the saloon interest. On the occasion of their fiftieth wedding anniversary, Adolphus Busch, "America's beer magnate, who has taken bread from a million children and clothed a million mothers in rags," presented his wife with a golden tiara. J.F. Love warned that Busch was attempting the "crowning of the first American queen with the price of virtue." More appalling still was the fact that both a sitting and a former president had sent gifts. "Mr. Taft remembered his friend, Mr. Busch, and forgot the proprieties of his high office and sent twenty dollars of American money in an ivory box, and Mr. Roosevelt sent a gorgeous loving cup," the *Standard* reported. "Presidents are made and unmade by the whisky and Roman Catholic vote of this nation and no one knows this so well as the men who sent Mr. Busch these love tokens." Editor Gambrell wrote that it was a "public humiliation to see the president, and the ex-president, bowing down and worshiping the golden calf in a beer garden." It was an occasion not only for humiliation but for decisive action. The saloon threatened democratic government.[23]

At times the progressive rhetoric combined with religious fervor to produce images of Manichean conflict. "The festering and capacious maw of the whisky interest is not satisfied by its successes in having its friends, agents and representatives in the executive and legislative branches of your State government," cautioned Colonel T.N. Jones. "It has with . . . expert care reached out its slimy and corrupt fingers to place on the courts of this State those who are liberal in their views with reference to the whisky traffic and the saloon." Accusations abounded in the *Standard* that the "gigantic liquor trust" was a "mighty system," "the most appalling barrier to our modern civilization," "the most powerful and effective organization the world has ever known." It threatened the fundamental principles of civil government: "A struggle for civic virtue such as the world has never before witnessed awaits us." It was obvious to the Baptists on which side of this conflict stood the saloon keeper; he was "an anarchist in the Kingdom of God." If the prohibition amendment were to go down in defeat, "every evil spirit will be glad, and reinvigorated, the powers of darkness will break forth on every side to overrun the country." This was apocalyptic progressivism.[24]

The twentieth-century prohibitionists continued to express their concern regarding the threat from "foreigners." Like their predecessors, they did not nicely differentiate German Texans, Tejanos, and recent immigrants. They compounded this xenophobia with a virulent anti-Catholicism. This was consistent with the rhetoric of the earlier campaigns, but it also reflected the anti-foreign, anti-Catholic bias of many twentieth-century progressives, and of prohibitionists nationally. Fred Hale assailed the Liquor Dealers' Association of America, reminding *Standard* readers that "most of them are foreigners, who have but one plank in their political platform." And because they were also predominantly Catholic "they have no conscience in this business, believing they can be prayed out of purgatory." Editor Gambrell anticipated the arguments of partisans who would on the eve of national prohibition conclude with him that "the saloon is a foreign institution in spirit and in form . . . foisted on the American commonwealth as a means of raising revenues for war purposes." Two weeks later he attacked the "Mexicans, and in general, the unseasoned Americans, the people who have come from foreign shores and have their un-American ways and ideas in our country and hope to foreignize the Americans." Prohibition was a means to assimilate this threat before the foreigners could assimilate native Americans into their ranks. More significantly, prohibitionists were no longer defending a region from outsiders, but a nation. They were no longer campaigning as the best Southerners, but as the best Americans.[25]

Race continued to play a role in the twentieth-century prohibition campaign. Indeed, throughout the South, racial fears and hatred were being exploited with increasing success by white politicians in the early years of the century. Nevertheless, Texas prohibitionists remained ambivalent about the role of African Americans. The black vote was not as critical an issue in the 1911 campaign as it had been earlier, due to changes in the demographics in the state and political restrictions on African American voting rights. African Americans made up a smaller proportion of the total vote. Still, voting as a bloc they could influence the outcome of the election. Certainly prohibitionists were critical of African Americans who opposed prohibition. The *Standard* reported that the leader of the "negro contingent" to the Statewide Saloon Rally "told the negroes that the reason he was opposed to Statewide prohibition was because they wanted their liquor cheap." More often, however, African Americans were portrayed as a group victimized by the saloon. They might be persuaded that it was in their best interest to support prohibition. "Saloons brutalize and profligate blacks and white women suffer from their outrages," the *Standard* warned. "In turn law and order suffers, as was shown in Dallas some time back when a mob hung a Negro, in open daylight, at a public street crossing." The Anti-Saloon League's *Home and State* sounded the same theme. Appealing for their votes, the paper reminded African Americans that "along with the saloon goes the rapist, and along with he rapist goes the mob." Such unfortunate events could be prevented by removing the temptation of the saloon. African Americans unsure as to how to vote on the issue were to understand that a vote for prohibition could translate into a vote against lynching.[26]

The editor of the *Standard* recognized the significance of the African American voter at the beginning of the campaign. "Everybody knows, in advance, that the Negroes will play an important part in the coming amendment campaign," he acknowledged. "The liquor men are counting on them and are right now working with all deceivableness and cunning craftiness to use them to perpetuate their business." But while Gambrell admitted that the liquor interests "will get many of them, the low, debased, and vicious," he asserted, "they will not anything like get all of them; not the most of them, if we will do our duty."[27]

Gambrell expressed optimism that the campaign could be pitched successfully in the black communities. "I have been in more than 50 prohibition campaigns and I know that the negroes can be largely appealed to by a straight-forward, open, direct approach," he wrote. "Every negro voter in your community ought to be seen personally." Yet simple electioneering might not be sufficient to guarantee a dry vote from the African Americans. "Uncommon efforts will be made to corrupt the negroes with money," Gambrell warned. "The right kind of committee in each community can prevent this." The ambiguity of the advice could allow readers to interpret this as a call to be vigilant that bribes were not offered, but it could also be read as an endorsement of coercion.[28]

The prohibitionists encouraged black leaders to work with them in the amendment campaign. "The best negroes and the best whites owe it to the situation to see that the negroes are not driven like dumb cattle and voted for whisky," the *Standard* admonished. The paper reported that "the negro race is furnishing many noble temperance workers." It quoted one who was fighting to "free our race of the second slavery — whisky." Indeed, the *Standard* provided a platform for black ministers and prohibitionists throughout the campaign. When the Colored Pastors' Association of Galveston resolved "in favor of the utter extermination of the liquor traffic from the State of Texas," the *Standard* printed the full text of the resolution with approving commentary. And when the paper provided space for the Negro Statewide Prohibition Association to publish an appeal, Gambrell asked "every white reader to read it and consider it."[29]

This extraordinary endorsement went to the Rev. J.W. Bailey, chairman of the Association, and his appeal merits closer examination. Bailey headed a delegation of black prohibitionists to the Fort Worth meeting of the Statewide Prohibition Amendment Association in December of the previous year. Like many who had attended that meeting, Bailey remarked on the spirit of unity and cooperation that had prevailed among the various groups represented. He recalled the slogan which appeared on badges worn by many of the delegates: "Every other issue under Heaven aside in 1911—I'm for State-wide Prohibition." But there is some indication that Bailey did not limit this offer of conciliation to interdenominational or theological questions, as did many present. "These are most significant words," Bailey wrote. "If Texas can rise up to the dignity of these wonderful words and really in spirit and in truth carry out the heaven-born idea herein expressed, the battle is already won." He was careful to affirm that he was a member of the "weaker race" and he even conceded that lynching was the result of saloons, although he did so with the important qualification that their impact was evident in "the mob" as well as in "the rapist." Clearly he was sensitive to the racial concerns and the racism of his white audience, and he tried to reassure them with language that would have recalled to those familiar with it Booker T. Washington's address at the 1895 Atlanta Exposition: "We are not seeking social equality. We do not want that and would not have it if it were offered to us." Still, he asserted that the meeting represented "moral purity and civic righteousness for all the people of every nationality without regard to race or color, creed or political affiliation."[30]

Bailey was quite aware of what was at stake for the African Americans in this campaign. "The negro helped in the freedom of the body in 1865 and wants to help in the glorious freedom of the soul in 1911," he wrote. "He has had an active part in the glorious work of Prohibition thus far waged in this country and does not want to be eliminated." In the issue of the *Standard* printed two days before the vote Bailey was more explicit in his appeal. "I again urge my race to be at the polls July 22nd, and cast their votes for the amendment," he pleaded. "The negro voters are now on trial." The *Standard* editors frequently praised Bailey and his colleagues for their leadership. "The Negroes have acted with good sense in organizing among themselves, for the great struggle we are to have," Gambrell wrote. "They have noble leaders, able and true men and women, who labor under a deep sense of race responsibility."[31]

Even before the final vote was tallied on the amendment, there was evidence that Bailey and Gambrell were to be disappointed in their expectations of support among African Americans. Texans voted on July 22, and the July 27 edition of the *Baptist Standard* went to press before the final count was completed. Statewide Prohibition Chairman Thomas Ball was quoted in the paper expressing guarded optimism. "In spite of wholesale fraud in various sections of the State in poll tax payments by liquor interests and a practically solid Mexican vote and 85 per cent of the negro vote against the prohibition amendment," Ball judged that "prohibition has been carried by not less than 10,000 majority." Two weeks earlier J.B. Gambrell had predicted a margin of victory of 50,000 votes, but now he concurred in Ball's more conservative estimate. He hoped that a greater number of black voters had supported the amendment, but was troubled by reports that they had not. "The thing happened that was to be feared the whole time," he lamented. "Whole communities of negroes were so fixed privately, after the old carpet-bag style, that nobody could get a hearing." Having raised the specter of Reconstruction, Gambrell continued the analogy. "The older readers of the *Standard* will remember the days of confusion during the reign of the carpet baggers, and how at last it was developed beyond doubt that the plan was for a few men—some carpet-baggers, some scalawags—to mass all of the negroes in silent battalions, and with the saloon element, force carpet-bag rule on the people." As his confidence in a decisive victory began to wane, Gambrell recalled the confusion and humiliation of the defeated white Southerners, and belatedly returned to the regionalism of the earlier campaigns. The recollection may have resonated with many of his prohibitionist readers as a postmortem, but it was too late for the campaign.[32]

When the final vote was tallied, the voters of Texas had rejected statewide prohibition by 213,096 to 237,393. Prohibition was defeated by a margin of just over five percent of the nearly half million votes cast. The post-election analysis of the *Standard* reflected a greater emphasis on race than had the campaign itself. More frequently the African Americans were blamed for the failure of the amendment and it is clear that the Baptists had in mind a different strategy for the next campaign. "If negroes degrade citizenship, while they have citizenship rights, they lower the level of our civilization," Gambrell warned. "We must look this matter straight in the face and meet it like the Anglo-Saxon race has met every great issue." It is not certain that Gambrell had in mind the immediate disfranchisement of African Americans. "We must help the negroes up," he continued, "not for our sake only, but for ours and all the generations to come." Former editor James B. Cranfill, who had penned the inflammatory editorial "The Native White Man" a quarter of a century earlier, was less conciliatory. "A generation of negroes has come upon the scene who never knew what slavery was, and who never felt the kindly influence of the Christian slave-holder, and thus learned to love the whites," he asserted. As a result "there has grown up a spirit of rebellion among some of the blacks against the white people that bodes no good for either race." Cranfill argued that the white voters had paid too little attention to the potential power of the black vote. "When we have another prohibition election," he wrote, "I trust those who are chosen to lead the campaign will have a care for this important matter." The editor of the Anti-Saloon League's *Home and State* warned that African Americans who opposed the amendment "will learn better bye and bye." He recommended an "educational qualification" for voters. Two years later, the legislature passed a literacy test for all voters in general elections in Texas. Governor Oscar Colquitt, who had won reelection in 1912 in a race against prohibitionist Democrat Thomas Ball, vetoed the measure.[33]

In the campaigns of the 1880s male prohibitionist leaders had increasingly distanced themselves from their female predecessors. This process culminated in the 1911 campaign, when women were practically invisible throughout. The Statewide Prohibition Campaign Committee published the itinerary of prohibitionist speakers in the field three weeks before the vote. All were male. Women continued to hold vigils in front of saloons and at the polls on election day, continuing the practice of treating voters with sandwiches, pie, and fresh water; but they had little role in the planning and execution of the prohibition campaign. Occasionally women would merit brief attention in the press, such as the notice in the San Antonio *Daily Express,* "the women will hold a meeting in the airdome, the prohibition grounds." In a lengthy speech a week before the vote, former Governor Thomas Campbell praised the women working for prohibition, but mentioned neither specific individuals or organizations. Within a few years women would be again at the center of the prohibition debate as national prohibition and female suffrage converged, but in 1911 they most often merited mention in the Texas press as helpless victims, along with children, of the insidious saloon. The Texas WCTU was still functioning under the leadership of state President Nannie Webb Curtis, but the organization generally did not play a significant role in the campaign. Prohibitionist H.A. Ivy commented, "it has not been so necessary for the W.C.T.U. to take such an active hand as formerly in securing temperance legislation, as the men have largely relieved them of that task." Female prohibitionists were expected to function as a ladies' auxiliary to the male organizations. A generation earlier male prohibitionists had equivocated; they had initially welcomed the women of the WCTU, but then began to distance themselves from their female counterparts out of fear that association with women reformers would make them vulnerable to criticism from opponents who would charge them with consorting with the "short-haired women" of the north. By 1911 they could reject the assistance of the women because they were confident that they could accomplish their goal without them.[34]

The prohibitionists of the 1880s were keenly aware that theirs was a fledgling movement. They struggled with the place of that reform in a society that was suspicious of their claim of authenticity. They responded by casting themselves and their cause as genuinely southern and particularly Texan. They rejected potential allies who might cast doubt on their authenticity, and stressed their own regional loyalties and culture. Most of them avoided association with prohibitionists in other states, except those of the former Confederacy, and denied having national aspirations. By 1911 this initial insecurity had passed and no longer shaped the organization and strategies of the movement. The Texas Anti-Saloon League was one state chapter of a larger national organization. The prohibitionist Democrats identified themselves with the progressive wing of the national party. Statewide prohibition was but one step in a process that had implications for the entire nation; it was not a process intended to culminate simply in a reformed Texas.[35]

In 1887 prohibitionists defended their honor to defend their southern authenticity and to legitimize their claim to speak as Texans. In 1911 there was little mention of honor. But in one letter to the editor of the *Texas Christian Advocate*, a writer echoed the appeals of an earlier generation. Mrs. J.T. Griswold, President of the Northwest Texas Conference of the Methodist Women's Home Missionary Society castigated the male prohibitionists for refusing women the ballot when "the vilest negro that walks the streets" was able to vote for the saloon. "Men of the Southland, what has our womanhood always done in time of trouble?" she asked, and then provided the response: "She has appealed to you and Southern chivalry has never failed." She could only hope that men would do the honorable thing. In a separate incident, an appeal to honor was made after the election was over. Jacob Wolters, a leader of the anti-prohibitionist forces was called before the Texas legislature to answer charges that the antis had illegally paid poll taxes and had thereby stolen the election. Wolters objected to this attack on his honor. In response, J.H. Gambrell of the Anti-Saloon League expressed his skepticism regarding Wolters motives. "When a man poses as supersensitive about his personal honor, but helps to involve his entire State in dishonor, he puts himself under grave suspicion," he wrote. "Men involved in questionable transactions cannot bully themselves out of them by vaunting their 'personal honor.'" To Gambrell, Wolters' appeal to honor had been disingenuous, even anachronistic.

Texans eventually chose prohibition, voting in 1919 (overwhelmingly, but with extraordinarily low turnout) for statewide prohibition in advance of the adoption of the Eighteenth Amendment to the U.S. Constitution. But the issue had become a national one, and the success in Texas had become a minor chapter in the national history of prohibition. In 1919 Texans voted for prohibition for the same reasons that Americans (or more often their state legislators) did: The triumph of progressivism, the attack on the liquor trust, and the xenophobia of the First World War. The reform that succeeded was the same reform that had failed in Texas three decades earlier. But there was less at stake. In the twentieth century prohibition was a policy question. In the 1880s, for Texas prohibitionist, it had been a matter of identity.

Notes

Introduction

1. Eben Lafayette Dohoney, *The Constitution of Man in the Physical, Psychical, and Spiritual Worlds* (Denver, CO: Reed Publishing Co., 1903), 217–18. An earlier version of this chapter appeared as "The Lone Star State Surrenders to a Lone Woman: Frances Willard's Forgotten 1882 Texas Temperance Tour," *Southwestern Historical Quarterly* 102, no. 1 (July 1998): 45–61.
2. On the connection between Spiritualism, reform, and feminism, see Ann Braude, *Radical Spirits: Spiritualism and Women's Rights in Nineteenth-Century America*, 2nd ed. (Bloomington: Indiana University Press, 2001).
3. Richard Hofstadter, *The Age of Reform: From Bryan to F.D.R.* (New York: Random House, 1955), 289–92; Joseph R. Gusfield, *Symbolic Crusade: Status Politics and the American Temperance Movement* (Urbana: University of Illinois Press, 1963), 7, 9–10; K. Austin Kerr, *Organized for Prohibition: A New History of the Anti-Saloon League* (New Haven: Yale University Press, 1985), John J. Rumbarger, *Profit, Power, and Prohibition: Alcohol Reform and the Industrialization of America, 1800–1930* (Albany: State University of New York Press, 1989); Anne Firor Scott, *The Southern Lady: From Pedestal to Politics, 1830–1930* (Chicago: University of Chicago Press, 1970); Janet Zollinger Giele, *Two Paths to Women's Equality: Temperance, Suffrage and the Origins of Modern Feminism* (New York: Twayne Publishers, 1995); Morton Keller, *Affairs of State: Public Life in Late Nineteenth Century America* (Cambridge, MA: Harvard University Press, 1977), 128–31, 512–14, 569–70; Paul Kleppner, *The Cross of Culture: A Social Analysis of Midwestern Politics, 1850–1900* (New York: Free Press, 1970), 144–46; Richard Jensen, *The Winning of the Midwest: Social and Political Conflict, 1888–1896* (Chicago: University of Chicago Press, 1971), 58–88; Norman Clark, *Deliver Us From Evil* (New York: W.W. Norton, 1976).
4. Many of these recent studies focus on the politics of North Carolina. The most important is Glenda Elizabeth Gilmore, *Gender and Jim Crow: Woman and the Politics of White Supremacy in North Carolina, 1896–1920* (Chapel Hill: University of North Carolina Press, 1996). Also see Janette Thomas Greenwood, *Bittersweet Legacy: The Black and White "Better Classes" in Charlotte, 1850–1910* (Chapel Hill: University of North Carolina Press, 1994), and Eric Anderson, *Race and Politics in North Carolina, 1872–1901: The Black Second* (Baton Rouge: Louisiana State University Press, 1981). In a recent study, Judith N. McArthur demonstrates that reform-minded Texas women were not as successful until the federated club movement allowed women to couch their demands for a greater political voice in terms of an expanded domestic role, rather than the more radical egalitarianism of nineteenth-century feminists (*Creating the New Woman: The Rise of Southern Women's Progressive Culture in Texas, 1893–1918* [Urbana: University of Illinois Press, 1998]).

5. A good overview of drinking practices and consumption rates in America can be found in Mark Edward Lender and James Kirby Martin, *Drinking in America: A History*, rev. ed. (New York: Free Press, 1987). On the saloon as a social and political institution, see Perry R. Duis, *The Saloon: Public Drinking in Chicago and Boston, 1880–1920* (Urbana: University of Illinois Press, 1983) and Madelon Powers, *Faces Along the Bar: Lore and Order in the Workingman's Saloon, 1870–1920* (Chicago: University of Chicago Press, 1998).
6. *Eleventh U.S. Census* (1890), part III, p. 10.
7. For various interpretations of the shift in voter loyalty in the southern states in the 1960s and 1970s, see Merle Black and Earl Black, *Politics and Society in the South* (Cambridge, MA: Harvard University Press, 1987); Edward G. Carmines and James A. Stimson, *Issue Evolution: Race and the Transformation of American Politics* (Princeton, NJ: Princeton University Press, 1989); and Joseph A. Aistrup, *The Southern Strategy Revisited: Republican Top-Down Advancement in the South* (Lexington: University Press of Kentucky, 1996).

Chapter 1

1. Joseph E. Roy, "Miss Willard in Texas," *The Independent* (New York). Woman's Christian Temperance Union National Headquarters Historical Files (joint Ohio Historical Society–Michigan Historical Collections), *Temperance and Prohibition Papers*, microfilm ed., WCTU series [hereafter WCTU series], reel 30, scrapbook 7. The article was also reprinted in the *Union Signal* [Chicago], March 23, 1882.
2. War Department, Signal Service, Monthly Meteorological Reports, Denison, Texas, Jan. 1882; Galveston, Texas, Jan. 1882.
3. The best biography of Willard is Ruth Bordin, *Frances Willard: A Biography* (Chapel Hill: University of North Carolina Press, 1986); although Mary Earhart, *Frances Willard: From Prayers to Politics* (Chicago: University of Chicago Press, 1944) remains an important defense of the WCTU and a significant effort to place Willard as a leader in nineteenth-century feminist circles. Willard's autobiography, *Glimpses of Fifty Years: The Autobiography of An American Woman* (Chicago: Woman's Temperance Publication Assn., 1889) is detailed and fascinating, but suffers from being hurriedly pieced together and deals little with the southern tours. Also useful for insight into Willard's character is Carolyn De Swarte Gifford, *Writing Out My Heart: Selections from the Journal of Frances E. Willard, 1855–96* (Urbana and Chicago: University of Illinois Press, 1995), although Willard was not keeping a journal at the time of her Texas visit.
4. On the significance of Willard's southern tours see Ruth Bordin, *Woman and Temperance: The Quest for Power and Liberty, 1873–1900* (Philadelphia: Temple University Press, 1981), 76–85. On the complexities of engaging southern women in social reform the best work is still Scott, *Southern Lady*.
5. 196.2% as opposed to 89.1%. Char Miller and David R. Johnson, "The Rise of Urban Texas," in *Urban Texas: Politics and Development*, ed. Char Miller and

Heywood T. Sanders (College Station: Texas A&M University Press, 1990), 6.
6. The Methodist paper, the *Texas Christian Advocate*, on Jan. 28, 1882, published a detailed agenda of Willard's tour provided by the WCTU of Paris, Texas.
7. Willard's Texas tour merits a one-sentence mention in Alwyn Barr, *Reconstruction to Reform: Texas Politics, 1876–1906* (Austin: University of Texas Press, 1971), 86. Willard's visit is overlooked altogether in most general histories of the state; see, e.g., Rupert Richardson, Adrian Anderson, and Ernest Wallace, *Texas: The Lone Star State*, 6th ed. (Englewood Cliffs, NJ: Prentice Hall, 1993), 298; and David G. McComb, *Texas: A Modern History* (Austin: University of Texas Press, 1989), 134 (in which Carrie Nation is briefly featured). Willard's part in establishing the Texas WCTU is briefly noted in Ron Tyler, et al., eds., *The New Handbook of Texas* (Austin: Texas State Historical Assn., 1996), V:355. The date is incorrect.
8. Paris *North Texan*, May 13, 1882, WCTU series, reel 32, scrapbook 14, p. 144; Paris *North Texan*, May 20, 1881, WCTU series, reel 32, scrapbook 14, p. 140; E[ben] L[afayette] Dohoney, *An Average American; being a true history of leading events in the life of Lafayette, who was born in Ky.; but "went West to grow up with the country." Containing a brief outline of some of the decisive events of American history; with short sketches of representative men and women* (Paris, TX: E.L. Dohoney, 1907), 209–11; Seth Shepard McKay, ed. *Debates in the Texas Constitutional Convention of 1875* (Austin: University of Texas Press, 1930), 142–44; Ernest William Winkler, ed., *Platforms of Political Parties in Texas*. Bulletin of the University of Texas, no. 3 [1916] (Austin: University of Texas, 1916), 244; D. Leigh Colvin, *Prohibition in the United States: A History of the Prohibition Party and of the Prohibition Movement* (New York: George H. Doran Co., 1926), 169; *Union Signal*, Feb. 23, 1882.
9. *Union Signal*, Feb. 23, 1882; Galveston *Daily News*, Feb. 5, 1882; Feb. 7, 1882; Dallas *Texas Observer*, undated clipping in WCTU series, reel 13, scrapbook 15, p. 13; Jefferson *Daily Jimplecute*, Feb. 6, WCTU series, reel 32, scrapbook 15, p. 14.
10. Paris *North Texan*, Feb. 4, 1882, WCTU series, reel 32, scrapbook 15, p. 14; Frances Willard, *Woman and Temperance: or, The Work and Workers of the Woman's Christian Temperance Union* (Hartford, CT: Park Publishing Co., 1893), 574–79; Dohoney, *Average American*, 209–11; *Texas Tribune*, Feb. 16, 1882, WCTU series, reel 32, scrapbook 15, p. 14; Denison *Democrat*, Feb. 8, 1882, WCTU series, reel 32, scrapbook 15, p. 16.
11. Western Union telegram, Feb. 8, 1882, WCTU series, reel 12, folder 14. On Willard's relationship with her mother see Bordin, *Frances Willard*, esp. 123–24 and 185–86; and Willard, *Glimpses*, esp. 655–65.
12. *Tenth U.S. Census* (1880), *Population Statistics*, vol. 1, tables III and VIII; quotation from Houston *Daily Post*, May 1, 1882; Fort Worth *Democrat-Advance*, Feb. 12, 1882.
13. Denison *Democrat*, undated clipping, WCTU series, reel 32, scrapbook 15, p. 15; Sherman *Courier-Chronicle*, Feb. 12, 1882, WCTU series, reel 32, scrap-

book 15, p. 15. The reporter does not specify what portion of Joel 2, but there are some likely possibilities. There are two references to wine (Joel 2:19 and 2:24). And of course there is verse 28, which begins (in the KJV) "And it shall come to pass afterward, that I will pour out my spirit upon all flesh; and your sons and your daughters shall prophesy." Less likely did she refer to verse 20, beginning, "But I will remove far off from you the northern army, and will drive him into a land barren and desolate."

14. Denison *Democrat*, Feb. 8 and 11, 1882, WCTU series, reel 32, scrapbook 15, p. 16.
15. Paris *North Texan*, Feb. 4, 1882, WCTU series, reel 32, scrapbook 15, p. 14; Willard, *Woman and Temperance*, 574–79; Dohoney, *Average American*, 209–11; Texas *Tribune*, Feb. 16, 1882, WCTU series, reel 32, scrapbook 15, p. 14; Denison *Democrat*, Feb. 8, 1882, WCTU series, reel 32, scrapbook 15, p. 16; Anna Gordon to Mary Hill Willard, Feb. 14, 1882, WCTU series, reel 12, folder 14.
16. Sherman *Courier-Chronicle*, Feb. 12, 1882, WCTU series, reel 32, scrapbook 15, p. 15.
17. Austin *Statesman*, Feb. 23, 1882, WCTU series, reel 32, scrapbook 15, p. 23; Galveston *Daily News*, Feb. 24, 1882.
18. Frances Willard to Mary S. Hathaway, Feb. 23, 1882, reprinted in the Paris *North Texan*, undated clipping, WCTU series, reel 30, scrapbook 7. On Willard's emphasis on expansion and organization of the WCTU, and on Sallie Chapin's role in the southern states, see Bordin, *Woman and Temperance*, 72–94.
19. *Tenth U.S. Census* (1880), *Population Statistics*, vol. 1, table VIII; *Texas Siftings* (Austin), March 4, 1882, WCTU series, reel 32, scrapbook 15, p. 25;
20. *Texas Siftings* (Austin), March 4, 1882, WCTU series, reel 32, scrapbook 15, p. 25; San Antonio *Daily Express*, Feb. 24, 1882, WCTU series, reel 32, scrapbook 15, p. 24; Feb. 25, 1882, WCTU series, reel 32, scrapbook 15, p. 24; San Antonio *Evening Light*, Feb. 24, 1882, WCTU series, reel 32, scrapbook 15, p. 24 and 27; *Union Signal*, March 9, 1882; Galveston *Daily News*, Feb. 25, 1882.
21. San Antonio *Daily Express*, Feb. 25, 1882, WCTU series, reel 32, scrapbook 15, p. 24; San Antonio *Evening Light*, Feb. 25, 1882, WCTU series, reel 32, scrapbook 15, p. 25.
22. Frances Willard to Mary Hill Willard, Feb. 25, 1882, WCTU series, reel 12, folder 14.
23. Austin *Statesman*, Feb. 26, 1882, WCTU series, reel 32, scrapbook 15, p. 23; San Antonio *Daily Express*, Feb. 25, 1882, WCTU series, reel 32, scrapbook 15, p. 24.
24. Austin *Statesman*, Feb. 26, 1882, WCTU series, reel 32, scrapbook 15, p. 23; Galveston *Daily News*, undated clipping, WCTU series, reel 32, scrapbook 15, p. 23.
25. War Department, Signal Service, Monthly Meteorological Report, Galveston, Texas, Feb. 1882. On the distinctive culture of Galveston and the role of churchwomen in reform in the following decades see Elizabeth Hayes Turner, *Women,*

Culture, and Community: Religion and Reform in Galveston, 1880–1920 (New York: Oxford University Press, 1997).

26. Briggs transferred to the Texas Conference in 1878. Despite the fact that the city was not so predominantly evangelical, St. John's was the Methodists' flagship church in Texas. In 1878 the edifice was assessed at a value of $66,000, four times more than the next most valuable property in the Texas Methodist Conference. Macon Phelan, *A History of the Expansion of Methodism in Texas, 1867–1902* (Dallas: Mathis, Van Nort & Co., 1937), 143. Galveston *Daily News*, March 1, 1882; *Texas Christian Advocate*, March 4, 1882.

27. Houston *Daily Post*, Feb. 26, 1882, WCTU series, reel 32, scrapbook 15, p. 26; March 2, 1882, WCTU series, reel 32, scrapbook 15, p. 27; *Texas Christian Advocate*, March 4, 1882.

28. *Union Signal*, April 13, 1882; Galveston *Daily News*, Feb. 26, 1882; Fort Worth *Democrat-Advance*, Feb. 21, March 3, 7, 12, and 17, 1882; National WCTU minutes, 1885, p. 117, WCTU series, reel 2; May Baines, *A Story of Texas White Ribboners* (n.p., 1935), 23. On the importance of the WCTU in moving women into the ranks of social activism, see Barbara Leslie Epstein, *The Politics of Domesticity: Women, Evangelism and Temperance in Nineteenth Century America* (Middletown, CT: Wesleyan University Press, 1981), 115–46. For the experience of southern women in particular, see Scott, *Southern Lady*, esp. 135–63.

29. Gilmore, *Gender and Jim Crow*; Anderson, *Race and Politics*; Greenwood, *Bittersweet Legacy*. On the women of Tennessee, a good study is Marsha Wedell, *Elite Women and the Reform Impulse in Memphis, 1875–1915* (Knoxville: University of Tennessee Press, 1991). On Texas women see Turner, *Women, Culture, and Community*, and McArthur, *Creating the New Woman*.

30. Waco *Daily Examiner*, March 9, 1882; *Texas Christian Advocate*, March 4, 1882; Houston *Daily Post*, Feb. 19, 1882, WCTU series, reel 32, scrapbook 15, p. 26; Paris *Texas Tribune*, undated clipping, WCTU series, reel 32, scrapbook 15, p. 13; Fort Worth *Democrat-Advance*, Feb. 12, 14, 17, 24, and 25, March 16 and 23, 1882; March 3 and 7, 1882, March 1, 1882; National WCTU minutes, 1885, p. 117, WCTU series, reel 2. The success of local option prohibition was often very brief. As the state constitution allowed annual votes on the issue if citizens successfully petitioned, many counties remained dry for a year and then would vote wet in the next round of elections. Moreover, the report of twelve dry county votes, based on WCTU records, is difficult to verify. Local governments were not required to report the results of local option elections to the state. Previous historians and partisans have reported as few as three dry counties by 1887.

31. *Texas Christian Advocate*, Dec. 10, 1881, Feb. 4, 1882; Waco *Daily Examiner*, April 20, 1882; *Texas Prohibitionist*, Feb. 3, 1882, WCTU series, reel 32, scrapbook 15, p. 12. On the United Friends of Temperance in Texas, see H.A. Ivy, *Rum on the Run in Texas: A Brief History of Prohibition in the Lone Star State* (Dallas: Temperance Publishing Co., 1910), 19–23. On temperance movements in other southern states, see T.J. Bailey, *Prohibition in Mississippi, or, Anti-Liquor*

Legislation From Territorial Days, With Its Results in the Counties (Jackson, MS: Hederman Bros., 1917); James Benson Sellers, *The Prohibition Movement in Alabama, 1702–1943* (Chapel Hill: University of North Carolina Press, 1943); Daniel Jay Whitener, *Prohibition in North Carolina, 1715–1945* (Chapel Hill: University of North Carolina Press, 1945); C.C. Pearson and J. Edwin Hendricks, *Liquor and Anti-Liquor in Virginia, 1619–1919* (Durham, NC: Duke University Press, 1977); and Paul E. Isaac, *Prohibition and Politics: Turbulent Decades in Tennessee, 1885–1920* (Knoxville: University of Tennessee Press, 1965). Leonard Stott Blakey, *The Sale of Liquor in the South: The History of the Development of a Normal Social Restraint in Southern Commonwealths* (New York: Columbia University, 1912) is an early overview of the region. N.b., H.A. Ivy is no known relation to the present author.

32. *National Liberator* (undated clipping), WCTU series, reel 32, scrapbook 15, 43–44.
33. Galveston *Weekly News*, Feb. 16, 1882; Fort Worth *Democrat-Advance*, Feb. 18, 1882.
34. *State Gazette*, April 18, 1882, WCTU series, reel 32, scrapbook 15, p. 20; Fort Worth *Democrat-Advance*, April 19, 1882. Versions of the editorial also appeared in the Dallas *Times* and the Austin *Statesman*. Of course Texas Democrats were not the only southerners who recognized the threat female prohibitionists posed to the political order. Belle Kearney was an idealistic young teacher when she heard Willard speak in Jackson, Mississippi. She did not know of the WCTU until just before she attended the lecture, but was immediately drawn in and appointed state organizer within a month, becoming a successful lecturer for the cause throughout the South. She recalled: "Immediately upon entering the work of the Woman's Christian Temperance Union, I affiliated with the Prohibition party, as it was the only political body in the United States that stood for the protection of the home against the saloon. My brothers and I had stirring arguments on the subject." In their excitement they would walk rapidly up and down the long, old front gallery at the plantation home, and say, "You are the only one of a vast relationship who has gone over to a new political faith. If you and the women associated with you, continue the agitation that has begun you will eventually break up the Democratic party" (*A Slaveholder's Daughter* [New York, Abbey Press, 1900], 187–88).
35. Waco *Daily Examiner*, April 21 and 22, 1882; Fort Worth *Democrat-Advance*, April 23, 1882.
36. *Texas Christian Advocate*, Feb. 4, 1882. Willard quoted directly from the Home Protection resolution that the 1881 convention had passed without crediting herself for its authorship or passage and stressed that equal suffrage was only put forward as a drastic measure of last resort, when all other temperance efforts fail to produce results. "Beyond this no action was taken," she wrote, nor has the National Women's Christian Temperance Union ever done anything whatever in the line of work for woman's ballot, either partial or complete." She also reassured readers that she "never [has] spoken, either in public or private, in favor of

this branch of work for the women of the south." To the extent that this was true, it was a reflection of Willard's care to avoid jeopardizing the temperance cause by interjecting the divisive issue of suffrage at an inappropriate moment. Her letter to the *Texas Christian Advocate* was reprinted in the *Christian Advocate*, March 2, 1882, WCTU series, reel 32, scrapbook 15, p. 38. Willard was personally committed to the ballot for women and made every effort to gain its endorsement from the national Union. See Bordin, *Frances Willard*, 97–111. Denison *Democrat*, Feb. 12, 1882, WCTU series, reel 32, scrapbook 15, p. 19. It should be noted that despite the criticism of Willard on principle, the Democrat continued to publish news of her tour, and reactions from other papers, both favorable and critical.
37. On Carroll see Alan J. Lefever, *Fighting the Good Fight: The Life and Work of Benajah Harvey Carroll* (Austin, TX: Eakin Press, 1994).
38. *Texas Baptist*, March 9, 1882.
39. On the bi-racial female coalition and its demise, see Gilmore, *Gender and Jim Crow*.

Chapter 2

1. From J.B. Cranfill's report to the UFT at Waco, Waco *Examiner*, July 24, 1885.
2. *Texas Baptist*, July 9, 1885. The following year the two larger Baptist associations, the Baptist General Association and the Baptist General Convention of Texas, would combine and their two universities: Waco University and Baylor University at Independence, Texas, would merge and form Baylor University at Waco. Lefever, *Fighting the Good Fight*, 51–54. John W. Payne, Jr., "Richard Coke," *The New Handbook of Texas* (Austin: Texas State Historical Assn.), ii:193.
3. *Texas Baptist*, July 9, 1885.
4. Waco *Examiner*, June 21, 22, 24, 25, 26, 27, 28, and 30, 1885; *Texas Baptist*, June 30, 1885. A recent biography of Jones is Kathleen Minnix, *Laughter in the Amen Corner: The Life of Evangelist Sam Jones* (Athens: University of Georgia Press, 1993).
5. Dallas *Weekly Herald*, July 23, 1885; Waco *Examiner*, July 22, 23, and 24, 1885; Ivy, *Rum on the Run*, 19.
6. Waco *Examiner*, July 23, 1885; David M. Fahey, *Temperance and Racism: John Bull, Johnny Reb, and the Good Templars* (Lexington: University Press of Kentucky, 1996), 66–71.
7. Waco *Examiner*, July 23, 1885.
8. Ibid., July 22, 1885.
9. Ibid., July 24, 1885.
10. Ibid., Aug. 2, 1885.
11. Ibid.
12. Ibid.
13. For an application of this distinction in post-Reconstruction North Carolina, see Greenwood, *Bittersweet Legacy*.

14. Waco *Examiner*, Aug. 2, 1885.
15. Galveston *Daily News*, Aug. 11 and 12, 1885; Waco *Examiner*, Aug. 12 and 15, 1885.
16. Waco *Examiner*, July 25, Aug. 4, 5, and 12, 1885. Women were even less visible in the effort to defeat local option. The editor of the Waco Examiner reported one exception when the wife of Captain A.D. Storey presented the newspaper office with "a most magnificent anti-prohibition bouquet" (Waco *Examiner*, Sept. 2, 1885).
17. On Carroll's life and career, the best source is Lefever, *Fighting the Good Fight*. Also useful is James B. Cranfill, *Sermons and Life Sketch of B.H. Carroll* (Philadelphia: American Baptist Publication Society, 1893); and J.M. Carroll, *Dr. B.H. Carroll, The Colossus of Baptist History*, compiled and edited by J.W. Crowder (Fort Worth, TX: Seminar Hill Press, 1946).
18. Waco *Examiner*, Aug. 13, 1885.
19. Ibid., Aug. 14, 1885. All quotations from Coke's speech following appeared in the same article.
20. Coke's objections as a Southerner to prohibition and to clerical activism were in no way unique, and this of course helps to explain why they were so well received. A few days earlier the Waco *Examiner* had published an editorial in which the writer expressed a desire to "enter a plea against Puritanism, against the spirits of the Maflower [sic], and against the men today who would prescribe the functions of our common manhood as they and their descendants did under the blue laws of Connecticut two hundred years since." On the tension between notions of southern manhood and evangelical Christianity, see Ted Ownby, *Subduing Satan: Religion, Recreation, and Manhood in the Rural South, 1865–1920* (Chapel Hill: University of North Carolina Press, 1990). For the colonial and antebellum periods see Bertram Wyatt-Brown, *Southern Honor: Ethics and Behavior in the Old South* (New York: Oxford University Press, 1982), 103–5; Rhys Isaac, *The Transformation of Virginia, 1740–1790* (New York: W.W. Norton, 1982), 118–20 and 161–77; and Heyrman, *Southern Cross*, esp. 206–52.
21. Galveston *Daily News*, Aug. 21 and 22, 1885; Waco *Examiner*, Aug. 15, 18, 20, and 25, 1885; Aug. 23, 1885.
22. On Gibbs' views see Waco *Examiner*, Aug. 23 and 25, 1885, and Dallas *Daily Herald*, Aug. 29, 1885. Reagan quoted in Galveston *Daily News*, Aug. 21, 1885.
23. Mills' interview reprinted in Waco *Examiner*, Aug. 15, 1885.
24. Galveston *Daily News*, Aug. 11, 1885.
25. Galveston *Daily News*, Aug. 19, 1885; The *News* began to print regularly an entire page of correspondence on the prohibition issue. Waco *Examiner*, Aug. 29, 1885; *Texas Christian Advocate*, Aug. 22, 1885; Bonham *News* editorial reprinted in *Texas Christian Advocate*, Sept. 12, 1885.
26. Waco *Examiner*, Aug. 22 and 27, 1885; *Texas Christian Advocate*, Aug. 22, 1885. The Houston *Age* was one out-of-town paper that followed the Homan story. In an editorial, reprinted in Waco, the editor mused: "The papers have got a good

joke. Wm. K. Homan has been over at Waco making prohibition speeches, and telling the people what democracy is" (Waco *Examiner*, Sept. 1, 1885).
27. Waco *Examiner*, Aug. 2, 13, and 28, 1885.
28. Ibid., Aug. 26, 1885.
29. Galveston *Daily News*, Aug. 20, 1885.
30. Ibid.
31. Ibid.
32. Ibid.
33. Ibid.; *Texas Baptist*, Aug. 28, 1885.
34. Galveston *Daily News*, Aug. 29, 1885; Waco *Examiner*, Aug. 29 and 30, 1885; Dallas *Daily Herald*, Sept. 1, 1885.
35. Waco *Examiner*, Aug. 30, 1885.
36. Coke's remarks printed in the Dallas *Daily Herald*, Aug. 30, 1885; Waco *Examiner*, Aug. 30, 1885.
37. Dallas *Daily Herald*, Aug. 31, 1885.
38. Waco *Examiner*, Sept. 1 and 2, 1885; Dallas *Daily Herald*, Sept. 1, 1885; Galveston *Daily News*, Sept. 1, 1885; Austin *Daily Statesman*, Sept. 5, 1885; *Texas Christian Advocate*, Sept. 9, 1885.
39. Galveston *Daily News*, Sept. 2, 1885; Waco *Examiner*, Sept. 1, 2, and 13, 1885.
40. All quotes from, or reprinted in, *Texas Christian Advocate*, Sept. 12, 1885.
41. *Texas Christian Advocate*, Sept. 12, 1885.
42. Ibid., Aug. 29, Sept. 5, 1885; Galveston *Daily News*, Sept. 4, 1885; *Texas Christian Advocate*, Sept. 12, 1885.
43. The Galveston *Daily News* continued to provide the best statewide coverage of local option races through the fall of 1885. The Hempstead vote and funeral were reported in that paper on Sept. 12, 1885.

Chapter 3

1. *Texas Baptist and Herald*, May 18, 1887.
2. On the passage in the legislature of the amendment, see Galveston *Daily News*, Feb. 1, 25, and 26, 1887.
3. On the controversy regarding the scheduling of the vote, see Galveston *Daily News*, Feb. 26, 1887.
4. Frank L. Byrne, *Prophet of Prohibition: Neal Dow and His Crusade* (Gloucester, MA.: Peter Smith, 1969); Ernest H. Cherrington, *The Evolution of the Prohibition Movement in the United States of America* (Westerville, OH: The American Issue Press, 1920), 228–32; Robert Smith Bader, *Prohibition in Kansas: A History* (Lawrence: University Press of Kansas, 1986); Paul Isaac, *Prohibition and Politics*.
5. On the issue of judicial invalidation of local option election results in Hunt County (for one example) see the Dallas *Daily Herald*, Feb. 12, 1887. On the willingness of the prohibitionists to continue to press the issue after losing at the

polls, see the story reported in the Galveston *Daily News*, March 15, 1887 on the meeting to organize a summer campaign at the Temperance Hall in Ennis, Texas, the evening after the results were in on a failed local option campaign. On the antis' fears that a minority could maintain an unpopular prohibition amendment, see the Galveston *Daily News*, Aug. 1, 1887.

6. Galveston *Daily News*, Feb. 1 and 26, 1887; *Union Signal* (Chicago), March 10 and (quotation source) April 14, 1887.
7. The proceedings of the convention were widely reported across the state, with comprehensive coverage and favorable reviews even from editors that would refuse to endorse the amendment. The prohibitionist and religious press sent their own reporters, but also relied on stories reported by other papers' correspondents for details. See the Galveston *Daily News*, March 17, 1887; the *Texas Christian Advocate* (Galveston), March 24, 1887; and the Dallas *Daily Herald*, March 15 and 17, 1887.
8. *Texas Christian Advocate*, March 24, 1887; *Union Signal*, April 7, 1887.
9. *Union Signal*, April 7, 1887; Dallas *Daily Herald*, March 17, 1887; *Texas Christian Advocate*, March 31, 1887.
10. *Union Signal*, Jan. 27, 1887; *Texas Baptist and Herald*, June 8, 1887.
11. *Union Signal*, March 24, 1887; March 10, 1887.
12. *Texas Baptist and Herald*, July 13, July 6, April 27, 1887; Dallas *Daily Herald*, March 23, 1887. Paris *News* editorial reprinted in part in the Dallas *Daily Herald*, March 29, 1887. "Preachers and petticoats" caution from the Dallas *Daily Herald*, April 11, 1887.
13. The membership of the Executive Committee was listed in the *Texas Christian Advocate*, March 24, 1887, and only three members out of more than fifty appear with the title "Reverend" preceding their names. However, this does not accurately reflect the number of clerics on the committee. Only the Methodist clergy were identified by title; ministers from other denominations were listed by name only. One of the Methodists on the list was the Rev. George W. Briggs, a pastor of the First Methodist Church at Galveston and editor of the *Advocate*. The schedules for traveling clerics were printed frequently in the prohibitionist press, often with requests to aid in securing venues and lodging. See for example the tour of Dr. W.A. Jarrell of Dallas in the *Texas Baptist and Herald*, June 15, June 29, and July 6.
14. *Texas Baptist and Herald*, June 22, 1887; July 6, 1887. A.J. Holt to editor, *Texas Baptist and Herald*, June 22, 1887.
15. Dallas *Daily Herald*, March 4, 1887; San Antonio *Daily Express*, July 1, 1887; *Texas Baptist and Herald*, July 13, 1887; Galveston *Daily News*, July 31, 1887; Aug. 2, 1887.
16. *Texas Baptist and Herald*, March 23, 1887; Dallas *Daily Herald*, March 23, 1887; *Texas Baptist and Herald*, March 30, 1887. On evangelicals' initial opposition to and eventual accommodation with the slaveholders, see Heyrman, *Southern Cross*.
17. *Texas Baptist and Herald*, April 27, 1887; Dallas *Daily Herald*, May 4, 1887.

18. Dallas *Daily Herald*, May 4, 1887.
19. Broaddus was quoted in the *Texas Baptist and Herald*, May 4, 1887; Mills' speech was printed in the Dallas *Daily Herald*, May 9, 1887. On the continuing controversy surrounding clerical involvement in the campaign contrast the editorial "Preachers and Prohibition," *Texas Baptist and Herald*, May 25, 1887, and letters from "Salvian," San Antonio *Daily Express*, July 1, 1887 and "A Clergyman Who is a Total Abstainer," San Antonio *Daily Express*, July 3, 1887. Although Baptist ministers outnumbered clerics from other denominations in the state in 1887, on the stump they made up a majority out of proportion to their overall numbers, particularly in contrast to Methodists, who were usually just as likely to support prohibition. The congregational polity of the Baptist churches, allowing them to vote to permit their clergy time off for the campaign, and the fact that preaching was a part-time vocation for many of the denomination's clergy, probably account for the greater participation of Baptists on the stump for the reform.
20. *Texas Baptist and Herald*, July 6, 1887; Dallas *Daily Herald*, July 1, 1887; San Antonio *Daily Express*, July 7, 1887; Galveston *Daily News*, Aug. 2 and 3, 1887. Atlanta resolution printed in *Texas Baptist and Herald*, June 16, 1887.
21. Cranfill quote, *New York Voice*, Jan. 14, 1886; West quote, *Texas Baptist and Herald*, April 27, 1887; Reasoner on bloody shirt, Dallas *Daily Herald*, March 23, 1887; Barnett Gibbs on "short-haired men and long-haired women," Dallas *Daily Herald*, March 21, 1887; pamphlet report, *Texas Baptist and Herald*, Aug. 3, 1887.
22. *Texas Baptist and Herald*, June 15 and 29, 1887; Dallas *Daily Herald*, May 5 and 6, 1887.
23. *Texas Baptist and Herald*, July 20, 1887, April 13, 1887, and July 13, 1887; San Antonio *Daily Express*, July 5, 1887.
24. Sam Acheson, *35,000 Days in Texas: A History of the Dallas News and Its Forebears* (New York: Macmillan, 1938), 133; Ivy, *Rum on the Run*, 13; Rev. J.H. Stribling, D.D., "My Impressions of Rev. J.B. Link and his Work in Texas," in *Texas Historical and Biographical Magazine*, vol. 2, ed. J.B. Link (Austin, 1892), 603–8; Dallas *Daily Herald*, March 1, 10, 23, and 28, April 6 and 12, May 5, 12, and 18, 1887; *Texas Baptist and Herald*, March 16, May 4, June 1, 1887. Pickett's and Grubbs' pamphlets promoted in *Texas Baptist and Herald*, May 4, 1887. George C. Rankin, *Two Nights in the Bar-Rooms and What I Saw* (Nashville, TN: Southern Methodist Publishing House, 1887). Rankin's book was originally published for the Tennessee prohibition campaign, but was promoted and distributed in Texas for the amendment campaign. Street's itinerary printed in the *Texas Baptist and Herald*, June 22, 1887.
25. Dallas *Daily Herald*, May 5, 1887; Acheson, *35,000 Days in Texas*, 134–37.
26. For examples of ads, see the Dallas *Daily Herald*, March 12 and April 19, 1887; San Antonio *Daily Express*, July 5, 1887; *Texas Baptist and Herald*, April 13, 1887. The complaint on reduced revenue was printed in the Dallas *Daily Herald*, May 3, 1887.
27. Dallas *Daily Herald*, April 2, 1887; *Texas Baptist and Herald*, April 20, 1887; San

Antonio *Daily Express*, July 2, 1887; Galveston *Daily News*, Aug. 3, 1887; *Texas Baptist and Herald*, April 13, 1887, June 22, 1887; Galveston *Daily News*, Aug. 3, 1887.

28. Galveston *Daily News*, Aug. 3, 1887; San Antonio *Daily Express*, July 7, 1887; *Texas Baptist and Herald*, "The Saloons and Personal Liberty," March 16, 1887. For example, "The south has a vivid recollection of the pernicious growth of a kindred ism emanating from the same land of political preachers and strong-minded women, which cost the people millions and opened the way for radical misrule and the insidious advance of paternalism" (Galveston *Daily News*, Aug. 3, 1887). For a recent study of a particularly virulent attempt of a southern politician's response to threats on the political rights of white men from everyone from African Americans to former slaveholders, see Stephen Kantrowitz, *Ben Tillman and the Reconstruction of White Supremacy* (Chapel Hill: University of North Carolina Press, 2000).

29. *Texas Baptist and Herald*, July 20, 1887. In February of that year the United States Senate held hearings before the Senate Elections Committee investigating charges of intimidation of southern black voters. A delegation of twenty-five African Americans from Washington County, Texas traveled to the capital to testify before the committee. Their appearance was delayed by a memorial signed by eighty-five white citizens of Brenham and presented by Senator Richard Coke, a delay which allowed ex-Governor John Ireland to arrive in Washington with thirty white citizens to counter the testimony of the black Texans. Dallas *Daily Herald*, Feb. 15, 1887.

30. Dallas *Daily Herald*, April 11, 1887; May 5, 1887; *Texas Baptist and Herald*, April 27, 1887.

31. Dallas *Daily Herald*, May 5, 7, and 16, 1887; San Antonio *Daily Express*, July 6, 1887; Galveston *Daily News*, Aug. 3 and 4, 1887.

32. *Texas Baptist and Herald*, April 27, 1887; San Antonio *Daily Express*, July 2, 1887.

33. Rayner's letter was discovered by the anti-prohibitionists and reprinted in a number of papers, including the San Antonio *Daily Express*, July 27, 1887. On Rayner's career see David Gregg Cantrell, "The Limits of Southern Dissent: The Lives of Kenneth and John B. Rayner," Diss., Texas A&M University, 1988, esp. 246–51.

34. San Antonio *Daily Express*, July 27, 1887.

35. Cranfill's editorial appeared in the Waco *Advance*, May 26, 1887. Many writers failed to capitalize the word Negro. At times the intent was clearly racist, particularly when writers would refer to "Whites and negroes" or "negroes and Germans," but often it may have simply been a matter of common usage or inaccurate typesetting in newspaper offices. Rather than flag further occurrences with "[sic]," I have left the capitalization as it appeared in the primary source and will permit the reader to draw her own conclusions regarding the original writer's motives. The response appeared in the San Antonio *Daily Express*, July 7,

1887. Haygood's speech was reported in the Galveston *Daily News*, Aug. 1, 1887.
36. *Texas Baptist and Herald*, April 13, 1887.
37. San Antonio *Daily Express*, June 9 and 12, 1887; Dallas *Daily Herald*, April 5, 1887; *Texas Baptist and Herald*, July 27, 1887. The Rev. George Carstens reported that every member of his German Baptist church in Denton was a prohibitionist, *Texas Baptist and Herald*, July 13, 1887. Beauchamp's call for support for work among German Texans appeared in the *Texas Baptist and Herald*, July 27, 1887.
38. *Texas Baptist and Herald*, July 27, 1887; San Antonio *Daily Express*, July 7, 1887.
39. *Union Signal*, March 10, 1887; *Texas Baptist and Herald*, July 27, 1887; Dallas *Daily Herald*, May 19, 1887; Galveston *Daily News*, Aug. 4, 1887; *Texas Baptist and Herald*, July 6, 1887; Dallas *Daily Herald*, May 19, 1887; Feb. 16 and 18, and April 15, 1887.
40. *Texas Baptist and Herald*, May 4, 1887; Dallas *Daily Herald*, May 5, 1887; *Texas Baptist and Herald*, July 27 and Aug. 3, 1887.
41. Barr, *Reconstruction to Reform*, provides the best overview of the state's politics in the post-Reconstruction era.
42. Ibid., 86–87.
43. Dallas *Daily Herald*, April 11 and 13, 1887; *Texas Baptist and Herald*, June 1, 1887; Barr, *Reconstruction to Reform*, 89; San Antonio *Daily Express*, July 1, 1887.
44. Dallas *Daily Herald*, April 15 and 18, 1887; San Antonio *Daily Express*, July 3 and 27, 1887; Dallas *Daily Herald*, May 4 and 5, 1887; *Texas Baptist and Herald*, May 5 and 18, and July 6, 1887.
45. Dallas *Daily Herald*, July 1, 1887; San Antonio *Daily Express*, July 1, 2, 3, 5, 6, and 27, 1887; *Texas Baptist and Herald*, July 6 and 13, 1887; Galveston *Daily News*, July 31, Aug. 1 and 3, 1887. The rhetoric at the Carroll-Mills debate grew rather heated. At one point the congressman reportedly pointed to the cleric and declared, "Hell was so full of such preachers that their legs were sticking out at the windows." The prohibitionists capitalized on Mills intemperance for the remainder of the campaign. See in particular *Texas Baptist and Herald*, July 13, 1887.
46. Galveston *Daily News*, Aug. 3 and 4, 1887.
47. There was some controversy regarding the propriety of women at the polls. It appeared to some (particularly among the anti-prohibitionists) to be a precursor to female suffrage. See *Texas Baptist and Herald*, July 27, 1887 and Galveston *Daily News*, Aug. 2, 1887 for differing perspectives.
48. For various predictions see Dallas *Daily Herald*, March 21, April 12, and May 20, 1887; *Texas Baptist and Herald*, July 13 and 20, and Aug. 3, 1887; San Antonio *Daily Express*, July 27, 1887; Galveston *Daily News*, Aug. 3, 1887. Hayden quote from *Texas Baptist and Herald*, June 29, 1887.

Chapter 4

1. The particulars of the event have been pieced together from June and July, 1887 issues of the San Antonio *Daily Express*, the *Texas Baptist and Herald* (Dallas), the *Texas Christian Advocate* (Methodist; Dallas), the Galveston *Daily News*, the Waco *Day*, the Atlanta *Constitution*, and the North Topeka, Kansas, *Benevolent Banner*. The quote is from A.H. Sutherland to the editor of the San Antonio *Daily Express*, June 11, 1887.
2. Heyrman, *Southern Cross*. Also see Donald G. Mathews, *Religion in the Old South* (Chicago: University of Chicago Press, 1977); and Anne C. Loveland, *Southern Evangelicals and the Social Order, 1800–1860* (Baton Rouge: Louisiana State University Press, 1980). On the earlier clash of traditional southern and evangelical culture, see Rhys Isaac, *Transformation of Virginia*.
3. Turner had a long and distinguished, albeit somewhat idiosyncratic, career in the AME church. For a differing interpretations cf. William J. Simmons, *Men of Mark: Eminent, Progressive and Rising* (Cleveland: George M. Rewell, 1887), 805–19; Edwin S. Redkey, "Bishop Turner's African Dream," *Journal of American History* 54 (1967): 271–90; and John Dittmer, *Black Georgia in the Progressive Era, 1900–1910* (Urbana: University of Illinois Press, 1977), 5, 52–54, 69, 175–78.
4. San Antonio *Daily Express*, June 8, 1887.
5. A.H. Sutherland to editor, San Antonio *Daily Express*, June 11, 1887. Unlike most of the prohibition (and anti-prohibition leaders), Sutherland was a native Texan. His father had served as a private in the Texan army at San Jacinto. His uncle, Dr. John Sutherland, had been present at the siege of the Alamo in 1836, but had been sent out as a courier before the mission fell to Mexican forces. Dr. Sutherland's account of the battle has often been used by historians as a source for details of the event. It was finally published on the centennial of the battle. John Sutherland, *The Fall of the Alamo* (San Antonio: Naylor Co., 1936).
6. San Antonio *Daily Express*, June 9, 1887.
7. Kerrville *Eye* editorial reprinted in the San Antonio *Daily Express*, June 14, 1887; June 9, 1887.
8. For references to "long-haired men and short-haired women," see San Antonio *Daily Express*, July 6, 1887, and *Texas Baptist and Herald*, July 13, 1887. The prohibitionists could turn the tables on their opponents and cast them as the interlopers. A Fort Worth prohibition rally passed a resolution condemning the interference of "foreign brewers and distillers . . . with an honest Texas election" (San Antonio *Daily Express*, June 1, 1887). "Foreign" in this case meant from other states.
9. Edward L. Ayers, *Vengeance and Justice: Crime and Punishment in the Nineteenth-Century American South* (New York: Oxford University Press, 1984), 19. Much of the current analysis of honor is derived from the work of anthropologist Julian Pitt-Rivers, who developed his theories regarding honor in the study of Mediterranean cultures. Julian Pitt-Rivers defines honor as "the value of a per-

son in his own eyes, but also in the eyes of his society" ("Honour and Social Status," in *Honor and Shame: The Values of Mediterranean Society,* ed. J.G. Peristiany [Chicago: University of Chicago Press, 1966], 21). Elsewhere he writes of honor as "a sentiment, a manifestation of this sentiment in conduct, and the evaluation of this conduct by others, that is to say, reputation" ("Honor," *International Encyclopedia of the Social Sciences,* ed. David L. Sills [New York: Macmillan Co. & The Free Press, 1968], 6:503). Historian Bertram Wyatt-Brown, in his detailed analysis of southern honor, closely follows Pitt-Rivers when he describes honor as "the cluster of ethical rules . . . by which judgments of behavior are ratified by community consensus" (*Southern Honor,* xv). Edward Ayers, also in a southern context, is more succinct. He defines honor as "a system of values within which you have exactly as much worth as others confer upon you" (*Vengeance and Justice,* 3). In each case honor is regarded as a system of self-assessment in which the judgment of others is internalized. This assessment differs from a simple acknowledgment of social status, because what is at stake is not simply a person's place in society, but the perceived value of the individual. Other scholars do not make such a sharp distinction between honor and social status. See, e.g., Elvin Hatch, "Theories of Social Honor," *American Anthropologist* 9 (June 1989): 341–53.

Many scholars have observed that one distinguishing characteristic of societies in which honor is highly valued is a hierarchical social structure. Orlando Patterson argues that slavery often appears within the context of a timocracy, a society with an over-arching code of honor (*Slavery and Social Death: A Comparative Study* [Cambridge, MA: Harvard University Press, 1982], 77–101). Bertram Wyatt-Brown's analysis of the South leads him to the conclusion that "when a society has pretensions that there are no ranks, honor must necessarily be set aside or drastically redefined to mean something else" (*Southern Honor,* 14). That something else is "dignity," which Edward Ayers describes as "the conviction that each individual at birth possessed an intrinsic value at least theoretically equal to that of every other person" (*Vengeance and Justice,* 19). Other elements of an honorific society include a high regard for fidelity, courage, and masculinity, an obsession with female "purity," an extreme sensitivity to insult, and an appeal to an extralegal code of behavior to justify violence as a response to honor threatened. In an honorific society, all individuals may lay claim to honor, but from the perspective of a particular group in the society there must be those who fall outside of that claim, who have no honor, and who therefore cannot appeal to honor to claim injury and cannot be trusted to abide by its code of behavior.

10. On honor as an alienable right, see Frank Henderson Stewart, *Honor* (Chicago: University of Chicago Press, 1994).
11. San Antonio *Daily Express,* June 9, 1887.
12. The prohibitionists for their part suffered attacks only a few weeks following the egging incident when it became known that John Rayner, a black teacher and political activist, had gone so far as to offer advice to B.H. Carroll, the leader of

the prohibition campaign. Rayner wrote a letter to Carroll in March 1887, suggesting that the prohibitionists rely on the support of a few prominent black clergymen rather than employing every black minister that might seek work as a speaker. Although he never acknowledged the fact, Carroll evidently heeded the advice (Turner's visit was one indication). The anti-prohibition press had a field day with the letter. J.B. Rayner to B.H. Carroll (March 17, 1887), San Antonio *Daily Express*, July 27, 1887. The controversy is detailed in Cantrell, "The Limits of Southern Dissent," 247–50 and Gregg Cantrell, "'Dark Tactics': Black Politics in the 1887 Texas Prohibition Campaign," *Journal of American Studies* 25 (April 1991): 85–93. Cantrell cites a number of reprints of the letter in the Texas press.

13. John C. Willis finds a code of honor among slaves in antebellum Virginia, particularly among those who are not Christian; see "From the Dictates of Pride to the Paths of Righteousness: Slave Honor and Christianity in Antebellum Virginia," in *The Edge of the South: Life in Nineteenth-Century Virginia*, ed. Edward L. Ayers and John C. Willis (Charlottesville: University Press of Virginia, 1991), 37–55. Whether or not Turner felt the pressures of an honor code, southern whites would not likely have recognized his claim to honorable treatment. This ambiguous relationship between those within an honor group and those perceived to be outside of it is consistent with Frank Henderson Stewart's analysis of the anthropological literature. Stewart distinguishes two broad categories of honor: vertical and horizontal. Horizontal honor he defines as "a right to respect . . . that is due an equal" (*Honor*, 54). Relations between members of an honor group would be guided by the dictates of horizontal honor. Personal honor is a subset of horizontal honor distinguished by the fact that it is something that an individual can lose. In this case, personal honor would mean all claims to honor that an individual might make deriving from his status as a southern white male that other southern white males would be expected to recognize. An individual's personal honor would be jeopardized were he to take actions contrary to his group's code of honor, or if members of his honor group were to challenge his claim to honorable treatment. Vertical honor, refers to those claims to honor that involve individuals across honor group lines. This, according to Stewart, includes, but is not limited to "rank honor, . . . the honor that is enjoyed by all members of a superior rank in relations with their inferiors" (*Honor*, 54, 59). Chief Justice Roger Taney's assertion in *Dred Scott* that an African American "had no rights which the white man was bound to respect" is one illustration of the unidirectional nature of vertical honor.

14. Here Orlando Patterson's work on slaveholding societies is useful. Patterson found not only that slavery is commonly found in honorific societies, but that it is precisely here that freedom is held in such high regard (*Slavery and Social Death*, 334–42). A number of books chronicle the Southerner's response to national developments. Among the best are Steven A. Channing, *Crisis in Fear: Secession in South Carolina* (New York: W.W. Norton, 1974); William J. Cooper, Jr., *Liberty and Slavery: Southern Politics to 1860* (New York: Alfred A. Knopf,

1983); and John McCardell, *The Idea of a Southern Nation: Southern Nationalists and Southern Nationalism, 1830–1860* (New York: W.W. Norton, 1979).
15. For an important study of the efforts of white Southerners to find honor in defeat, see Charles Reagan Wilson, *Baptized in Blood: The Religion of the Lost Cause, 1865–1920* (Athens: University of Georgia Press, 1980).
16. For prohibitionist discussion of the "personal liberty" issue, see the Dallas *Daily Herald*, April 5, May 4, 5, 7, 9, and 12, 1887; *Texas Baptist and Herald*, April 13, 20, 27, May 18, June 1, 8, 15, 22, and 29, July 6, 20, and 27, Aug. 3, 10, 17, and 24, 1887.
17. San Antonio *Daily Express*, June 12, 1887.
18. Dallas *Daily Herald*, April 9, 1887; *Texas Baptist and Herald*, July 6, 1887.
19. *Texas Baptist and Herald*, July 13, 1887.
20. H.M. Du Bose, "The Model Saloon License League," *Nashville Tennessean*, June 14, 1908.
21. *Texas Baptist and Herald*, June 8, 1887; July 6, 1887. In July 1887 the Mississippi State Prohibition Committee met and passed a resolution remembering Gambrell as "a faithful, dauntless champion of moral, official temperance" (Bailey, *Prohibition in Mississippi* [n.p., 1917]).
22. "From its earliest days," Edward Ayers writes, "Southern evangelicalism defined itself in opposition to the culture of honor." While he acknowledges that as evangelicalism became the dominant variety of Protestantism in the South this opposition became less confrontational, he asserts that "the differences between Northern and Southern evangelicalism were scarcely greater than the differences between Southern evangelical piety and Southern honor." (*Vengeance and Justice*, 28). For the colonial period see Rhys Isaac, *Transformation of Virginia*. For a variation on this theme in the period addressed here, see Ownby, *Subduing Satan*. Ownby opposes southern evangelicalism and the culture of masculinity.
23. Bertram Wyatt-Brown in an article published since *Southern Honor* acknowledges this blending of the two systems. "The clergy and pious laymen were themselves part of the social regime that upheld the regional conventions and mores that the traditional ethic justified," he writes. "Many aspects of the ethical discourse were readily incorporated into Christian parlance and justification, a circumstance made easy by church and social tradition and by the narratives and codification of honor to be found in Scripture, particularly in the Old Testament" ("God and Honor in the Old South," *Southern Review* 25 [Spring 1989]: 283–84, 293–94). Nevertheless, he implies that prohibitionists would have abandoned this incorporation because they did not demonstrate the ambivalence characteristic of many Southerners regarding "sanctioned virility." On the evangelicals' critique, and subsequent appropriation, of elite culture see Heyrman, *Southern Cross*.
24. San Antonio *Daily Express*, June 12, 1887.
25. James B. Cranfill, *Dr. J.B. Cranfill's Chronicles: A Story of a Life in Texas Written by Himself about Himself* (New York: Fleming H. Revell Co., 1916), 311.
26. Ibid. Southern Baptist ecclesiology and rural southern realities also may help to

explain the ease with which Cranfill and others could reconcile the dissonant claims of culture and church. Baptist preachers, while ordained, rarely had much in the way of formal training. In fact, a congregation could "call" anyone they saw fit to serve as their pastor. Moreover, most rural ministers were paid so little that they generally were part-time preachers. That is, they farmed most of the week just like their neighbors. Each of these factors diminished the distinction between a clergyman and other men of honor.

27. Prominent black Texans were divided over the issue of prohibition. Supporters of the measure viewed enforced temperance as a means to encourage African Americans to work harder and to save their modest earnings. Particularly in the early twentieth-century campaigns some argued that the passage of the prohibition amendment would make it more difficult for whites to justify lynching as a means of controlling dangerous, drunken black males. For the most part, however, black Texans appear to have opposed prohibition. Contemporaneous post-election analysts on both sides of the issue credited the opposition of black voters for the defeat of the amendment in many counties. At least one recent scholar has corroborated these observations by means of a multiple-regression analysis of the 1887 vote. See Cantrell, "'Dark Tactics,'" 85.

28. Pitt-Rivers, "Honor," 506. Historian Clement Eaton writes of the southerner's concern with regional honor in the secession crisis as opposed to purely personal honor. Eaton confines the southern obsession with regional honor to a limited period from the debates over the Wilmot Proviso to the end of the Civil War. He sees it as an outgrowth of "a luxuriant romanticism of mind" that pervaded southern culture in the few decades preceding the secession crisis. He also recommends a reevaluation of honor in light of "the so-called realistic standards of the 'new morality.'" It is my position that honor as a cultural value is not so easily adopted or rejected. See Clement Eaton, "The Role of Honor in Southern Society," *Southern Humanities Review* 10 (1976, bicentennial supplement): 47–58. *Texas Baptist and Herald*, July 20, 1887. Most of the prohibition leaders in 1887 were not native Texans but were born in other southern states. Calvin Reasoner, a prominent stump speaker in the early days of the campaign had migrated to Texas from Kansas. When he was criticized as "that Kansas Republican," prohibitionists defended his right to participate at first, but eventually even prohibition papers began to call for him to take a lesser role. Dallas *Daily Herald*, March 1, 2, 4, 10, 12, 21, 23, and 24, and April 12, 1887; *Texas Baptist and Herald*, April 27, 1887.

29. *Texas Christian Advocate*, June 23, 1887.

30. For a contribution by an anthropologist to the study of "the cradle of Texas liberty," see Holly Beachley Brear, *Inherit the Alamo: Myth and Ritual at an American Shrine* (Austin: University of Texas Press, 1995), esp. ch. 3: "Texas in Her Birth," 23–44. *Texas Baptist and Herald*, Jan. 5, 1887 and May 25, 1887.

31. *Texas Baptist and Herald*, May 25, 1887. Burleson quotations that follow are from the same article unless otherwise noted. For an alternative epilogue to the story of Susannah Dickinson, suggesting that she followed a less-than-honorable

course to prostitution, see Jeff Long, *Duel of Eagles: The Mexican and U.S. Fight for the Alamo* (New York: William Morrow & Co., 1990), 339.

32. B.F. Riley, *History of the Baptists of Texas* (Dallas, TX: n.p., 1907), 308. In addition to drawing from Paul's mission to the Romans, Riley appears to have had in mind the apostle's efforts to preach in Jerusalem. In Acts 23, Paul is slapped in the face by the high priest Ananias when he tries to preach in that city. Both he and the Rev. Carroll were forced to appeal to the civil authorities for protection in the face of a hostile mob.

    Other prohibitionists found resonance in the efforts of the apostle Paul. A correspondent to the *Texas Baptist and Herald* during the campaign alluded to Paul's mission to the cities of Asia Minor when he wrote that "the rabble always fall in line when the cry is raised, 'Great is Diana of the Ephesians.'" Cf., Acts 19:22–41; S.J.A. to editor, *Texas Baptist and Herald*, June 29, 1887.

33. Martha E. Whitten, *Texas Garlands* (Austin, TX: Triplett & Hutchings, 1886), 345. In her poetry Whitten commonly used "dusky hordes" to refer to Indians, Mexicans, or African Americans. For her contribution to the prohibition campaign see Martha Whitten, *The Drunkard's Wife* (Austin, TX: Hutchings Printing House, 1887).

34. The battle over the history of the Alamo remains bitter and contentious. Critics of the Daughters of the Republic of Texas, the private organization entrusted with the maintenance of the site, point out that the organization has deemphasized, and at times ignored, the two-and-a-half century history of the mission before 1836, and the role of non-Anglo combatants in the Texas Revolution. Cf., Clara Driscoll, *In the Shadow of the Alamo* (New York: G.P. Putnam's Sons, 1906), Frederick C. Chabot, *The Alamo, Altar of Texas Liberty* (San Antonio, TX: n.p., 1931), Susan Prendergast Schoelwer, *Alamo Images: Changing Perceptions of a Texas Experience* (Dallas, TX: DeGolyer Library and Southern Methodist University Press, 1985), and Edward Tabor Linenthal, *Sacred Ground: Americans and Their Battlefields* (Urbana: University of Illinois Press, 1991), 53–86.

35. *Texas Baptist and Herald*, April 27 and April 13, 1887.

36. "The Battle Begun," *Texas Christian Advocate*, Aug. 4, 1887; *Texas Baptist and Herald*, June 1, 1887. Both prohibitionists and anti-prohibitionists echoed the rhetoric of an earlier revolution. A correspondent to the Texas Baptist and Herald wrote that those who opposed prohibition would eventually come to acknowledge the stakes in the battle and would "come, as did the heroes of 1776, pledging their lives and their fortunes and their sacred honor to the cause of Prohibition" (June 29, 1887). An anti-prohibitionist speaker in Galveston was even more eclectic in his sources. Arguing for "personal liberty," he declared that "we should look at the principle itself as a sacred one to be preserved and guarded, if need be, with our lives, our virtue [*sic?*] and our sacred honor, as one before which we will stand with uplifted arms facing the invader and warning him: 'Thus far shalt thou come, and no farther'" (Galveston *Daily News*, July 31, 1887).

Chapter 5

1. Roger Q. Mills quoted in the Dallas *Daily Herald*, May 9, 1887.
2. The accusation regarding ballots in Caldwell appeared as a letter to the editor in the Galveston *Daily News*, Aug. 7, 1887. The writer recommended that the legislature consider requiring standardized ballots in all future elections. The fraudulent voting accusations appeared in the Galveston *Daily News*, Aug. 5, 1887. On August 8 the paper reported that prominent citizens of El Paso held a rally and passed out handbills to dispute the allegations, pointing out that voter turnout in El Paso was not much higher in 1887 than in the previous year's general election. The quote from the WCTU member appeared in the Galveston *Daily News*, Aug. 6, 1887.
3. Galveston *Daily News*, Aug. 5, 1887.
4. Ibid.
5. Ibid., Aug. 5 and 6, 1887.
6. Ibid., Aug. 6 and 10, 1887; *Texas Baptist and Herald*, Aug. 17, 1887; Galveston *Daily News*, Aug. 7, 1887.
7. The 1887 election returns were printed in J.M. Moore, *Biennial Report of the Secretary of State of the State of Texas, 1888* (Austin, TX: State Printing Office, 1889), 146–48. Returns for many cities and towns were reported in the Galveston *Daily News*, Aug. 5, 6, and 7, 1887, and in the Dallas *Daily Herald*, Aug. 4 and 6, 1887. Fort Worth may have voted dry because of the publicity surrounding the murder of Texas Brewery Co. driver Mike Haggerty by a saloon keeper in the days prior to the vote. Richard F. Selcher, *Hell's Half Acre: The Life and Legend of a Red-Light District* (Fort Worth: Texas Christian University Press, 1991), 198–99. The Prohibition Executive Committee meeting was reported in the Galveston *Daily News*, Aug. 10 and 17, 1887.
8. *Union Signal*, Oct. 18, 1887.
9. *Texas Christian Advocate*, Aug. 18, 1887; Reagan letter reprinted in the *Texas Christian Advocate*, Aug. 18, 1887; Dallas *Daily Herald*, Aug. 5, 1887; *Union Signal*, Aug. 18, 1887.
10. Election returns were for the 1887 amendment vote were reported in Moore, *Biennial Report*, 146–48. Election returns for 1886 are from the State of Texas Secretary of State Register, RG 307, Election Registers, Archives and Information Services Division, Texas State Library and Archives Commission (hereafter ARIS-TSLAC). Census Data drawn from machine readable data from the Inter-university Consortium for Political and Social Research (ISPSR), Historical, Demographic, Economic and Social Data: The United States, 1790–1970, (ICPSR 003). When possible estimates were made for 1887 using census data from 1880 and 1890 and calculating for 1887 using the formula (0.7)(1880 data) + (0.3)(1890 data), and for 1886 using the formula (0.6)(1880 data) + (0.4)(1890 data). All data employed in calculations were county-level aggregate data. Correlation and regression calculations were made using SPSS for Windows 8.0. The results of these calculations are not the same as counted

votes; all numbers should be regarded as calculated estimates. There are now several texts available to assist historians in applying statistical methodology. Among the most useful are Roderick Floud, *An Introduction to Quantitative Methods for Historians* (London: Methuen & Co., Ltd., 1973 [2nd ed., 1979]); R. Darcy and Richard C. Rohrs, *A Guide to Quantitative History* (Westport, CT: Praeger Publishers, 1995); Konrad H. Jarausch and Kenneth A. Hardy, *Quantitative Methods for Historians: A Guide to Research, Data, and Statistics* (Chapel Hill: University of North Carolina Press, 1991); and Thomas J. Archdeacon, *Correlation and Regression Analysis: A Historian's Guide* (Madison: University of Wisconsin Press, 1994).

11. Eligible voters were divided into three groups for the first level of analysis. Corresponding to categories in population statistics in the 1880 and 1890 U.S. Census, they include native-born white males age twenty-one and over, foreign-born white males age twenty-one and over, and African American males (colored males in the U.S. Census) age twenty-one and over. Approximate population totals for 1887 were derived by calculating the average annual increase from the 1880 to the 1890 census. Participation of each group was calculated by means of multiple regression, weighing the cases by the estimated number of voters statewide. The number of eligible voters for each year was estimated by calculating from the number of males over twenty-one years of age reported in the 1880 census (379,482) and the number reported in the 1890 census (526,776) an average annual increase in the number of eligible voters of 14,729. A linear, rather than a logarithmic increase was assumed because most of the population increase was due to migration. This provides an estimated total of 467,856 eligible voters in 1886 and 482,587 voters in 1887. The estimated number of eligible voters in each county in 1887 is also used to weigh cases for correlation and regression calculations. Because of the problem of multicolinearity of the independent variables, calculations were made only on African American males and foreign-born white males. All correlations were significant at <.001. Inclusion of native white males introduced a zero-value divisor and made impossible the calculation of correlation coefficients. With estimated voter turnout as the dependent variable, the independent variable "percent African American eligible voters" yielded a zero-order correlation coefficient of .258 and a partial correlation coefficient of .187. The independent variable "percent foreign-born eligible voters" yielded a zero-order correlation coefficient of -.548 and a partial correlation coefficient of -.526. Since the total number of votes cast was known, and the totals for each category of eligible voters had been estimated, the calculations provided the totals of participating African American and foreign-born voters. The totals and percentages for native white voters could be calculated from these figures.

12. On the high level of participation by southern black voters in the 1880s, see J. Morgan Kousser, *The Shaping of Southern Politics: Suffrage Restriction and the Establishment of the One-Party South, 1880–1910* (New Haven, CT: Yale University Press, 1974), 14–28. It is likely that the numbers presented in Table

5.1 are accurate, but it would be a mistake to accept them as entirely precise. They are based on calculations that necessarily include estimates, and there are two other factors that affect their reliability. First, while there is a significant correlation among the variables, the two independent variables in the equation can explain less than two-thirds of the variation in total voter turnout at the county level ($R^2 = .636$). Variables other than the race and nativity of the voter also influence the level of participation, and these variables could have had an asymmetric influence on black and white voters. Second, there is the possibility that the results are compromised by the ecological fallacy: the assumption that the various groups of voters in each county turned out at approximately the same rate. It might be, for example, the a higher voter turnout in counties with more black voters was partly a result of greater participation by white voters who were motivated by fears of the political power of African Americans. Nevertheless, the overall high turnout in the 1887 election (except in several southern counties in the state), the similarity of participation figures for other elections in the decade, and the correspondence of these numbers with Kousser's (*Shaping of Southern Politics*) and contemporaneous observers weigh in favor of the table's reliability. The participation of foreign-born white males may be somewhat understated because the number of individuals born in Mexico was concentrated in the southern counties of the state where overall turnout was particularly low. However, because of the sparse population in many of these counties, the impact on aggregate voter turnout would not be particularly significant. It should also be noted that foreign-born voters were not necessarily citizens. Foreign-born males were eligible to vote if they declared their intention to become citizens at some future date.

13. The black vote was calculated by means of multiple regression using the percentage of votes for prohibition as the dependent variable and the numbers of African American and foreign-born white males expressed as percentages of eligible voters as independent voters. Cases were weighted by the number of votes cast. To account for differences in voter turnout, the partial correlation coefficients were adjusted by the following calculation: (mean voter turnout/variable voter turnout)(partial correlation coefficient). The result provides the likely difference from mean (36.9371%) in votes for prohibition. All correlations were significant at <.001. Nevertheless, the calculation yielded an impossible result in the case of foreign-born voters (with 122.3% voting against prohibition). This is not surprising. Almost all of the foreign-born Texans were natives of either Germany or Mexico. The Germans were concentrated in south-central Texas and in a few older counties of the coastal plains; the Mexicans lived mostly in the southern counties, areas where their countrymen had settled in previous generations (or in the case of Mexicans, where the border had migrated to them). These native Texans (all native white in the census reports) would be much more likely to oppose prohibition than the native white males of the rest of the state, and would have the effect of further concentrating the vote against prohibition in precisely those places where there was a higher concentration of immigrants.

A second calculation was made using native white males and foreign-born white males as the independent variables, and the results were utilized in determining the foreign-born vote for prohibition. Because there was a significant negative correlation between the percentage of African American and foreign-born males across counties, the corrected values would have little bearing on the initial calculation of the black vote. The remainder, after all African American and foreign-born votes were accounted for, would be the native white vote.

14. The regression equation yielded an R^2 of .684. All correlations were significant at <.001. The independent variable "percent born in other southern states" yielded a zero-order correlation coefficient of +.722 and a partial correlation coefficient of +.195. The independent variable "percent born in Texas" yielded a zero-order correlation coefficient of -.447 and a partial correlation coefficient of -.218. Because the calculations included an independent variable for African American voters, the partial correlation coefficients for southern and Texas nativity are corrected for the proportions of African Americans in that population. Figures for southern nativity were drawn from the 1880 census. As there was likely a proportionally greater increase in white migration than black to Texas between 1880 and 1887, the percentage of white Southerners voting for prohibition may be slightly overstated. The actual percentage would still be very close to 57%, and there is no accurate way to calculate the possible discrepancy. Approximately 13% of Texans were born in northern states. A separate calculation using that population as a variable finds no significant correlation (partial correlation = -.001) between the northern nativity and support for prohibition when all other possible birthplaces are included as variables.
15. Maps generated using AniMap Plus County Boundary Historical Atlas version 2.0.1.
16. Correcting for the seven-year difference in data in the two maps would likely cause an increase in the correlation. As new Texans moved into the state, they would have settled farther west, and as the southern-born population of the eastern counties aged, the percentages born outside of the state would have declined. On southern migration into the state, see D.W. Meinig, *Imperial Texas: An Interpretive Essay in Cultural Geography* (Austin: University of Texas Press, 1969), esp. 42–46.
17. This is not to imply that Texas was an egalitarian, nonracist society or even that all Texans received equal treatment under the law. Tejanos in particular suffered discrimination and dispossession throughout the century. See Arnoldo De Leon, *The Tejano Community, 1836–1900* (Albuquerque: University of New Mexico Press, 1982); Arnoldo De Leon, *They Called Them Greasers: Anglo Attitudes Toward Mexicans in Texas, 1821–1900* (Austin: University of Texas Press, 1983); and David Montejano, *Anglos and Mexicans in the Making of Texas, 1836–1986* (Austin: University of Texas Press, 1987). On German Texans see Glen E. Lich, *The German Texans* (San Antonio: University of Texas Institute of Texan Cultures at San Antonio, 1981); for a more localized study, see Walter Struve, *Germans and Texans: Commerce, Migration, and Culture in the Days of the Lone*

Star Republic (Austin: University of Texas Press, 1996). On the challenges faced by evangelical denominations trying to organize in Texas, see Howard Miller, "Texas," in *Religion in the Southern States: A Historical Study*, ed. Samuel S. Hill (Macon, GA: Mercer University Press, 1983), 313–33; Carter E. Boren, *Religion on the Texas Frontier* (San Antonio, TX: Naylor Co., 1968); Walter N. Vernon, et al., *The Methodist Excitement in Texas: A History* (Dallas: Texas United Methodist Historical Society, 1984), 152–201; and Robert A. Baker, *The Blossoming Desert: A Concise History of Texas Baptists* (Waco, TX: Word Books, 1970), 134–52.

18. At the national level and in many states there was a clear correlation between party loyalty and support of prohibition. Democrats, particularly where supported by a working class, immigrant, or Catholic base, tended to oppose prohibition. Republicans, heirs to the Whig reform culture and party of northern Protestants, generally supported it. In the southern states the Democratic Party was the party of white racial hegemony and the Republican Party was the party of the freedmen and of a variety of reformers and immigrant groups.

19. The calculation was made using Percent for Prohibition as the dependent variable and Percent Republican in 1886 and Percent Democratic in 1886 as the independent variables. Cases were weighted by total vote cast in 1887. The calculations yielded zero-order correlation coefficients of -.355 (Republican and Prohibition) and +.198 (Democratic and Prohibition). The partial correlation coefficients were -.406 for the Republican vote and -.286 for the Democratic. Another problem with the calculation was the overall explanatory power of the regression: $R^2 = .197$. That is, at the county level, variation in party affiliation in 1886 could not account for most of the variation in the prohibition vote, despite the overall significance of the calculations and the suggestive correlations. Other variables (e.g., race, ethnicity, and nativity) were better predictors than party affiliation of voting behavior in 1887.

20. Jefferson Davis to F.R. Lubbock, July 20, 1887, Texas State Library and Archives; San Antonio *Daily Express*, July 27, 1887.

21. *Texas Baptist and Herald*, Aug. 3, 1887; Reagan's letter was reprinted in the *Texas Christian Advocate*, Aug. 4, 1887.

22. All of these editorial snippets were reprinted in the *Texas Christian Advocate*, Aug. 18, 1887.

23. Galveston *Daily News*, Aug. 5, 1887; Barr, *Reconstruction to Reform*, 92; *Texas Christian Advocate*, Sept. 1, 1887. On the address of the Prohibition Executive Committee see *Texas Baptist and Herald*, Aug. 24, 1887 and *Texas Christian Advocate*, Sept. 8, 1887.

24. *Wesleyan Advocate* letter reprinted in the *Texas Christian Advocate*, Aug. 18, 1887; *Texas Christian Advocate*, Aug. 11, 1887; *Union Signal*, Aug. 18, 1887; *Texas Christian Advocate*, Aug. 4, 1887.

25. Jenny Bland Beauchamp, "The Lesson of the Defeat," *Texas Baptist and Herald*, Aug. 31, 1887.

26. Ibid.

Coda

1. San Antonio *Daily Express*, Aug. 8, 1903.
2. On the diminishing "southernness" of North Texas communities, see Walter L. Buenger, *The Path to a Modern South: Northeast Texas between Reconstruction and the Great Depression* (Austin: University of Texas Press, 2001).
3. Population statistics on Dallas are from Jim B. Pearson, et al., *Texas: The Land and Its People*, 2nd ed. (Dallas, TX: Hendrick-Long Publishing Co., 1978), 548.
4. Quoted in Lewis L. Gould, *Progressives and Prohibitionists: Texas Democrats in the Wilson Era* (Austin: University of Texas Press, 1973), 44.
5. See Lich, *German Texans*. Seth Shepard McKay, *Texas Politics, 1906–1944, with Special Reference to the German Counties* (Lubbock: Texas Tech University Press, 1952) has an extended discussion of the political significance of the German Texans.
6. On the Tejanos, see in particular De Leon, *Tejano Community*; De Leon, *They Called Them Greasers*; and Montejano, *Anglos and Mexicans*.
7. For differing perspectives on the aims of the prohibitionists nationally in these years see Jack S. Blocker, Jr., *Retreat From Reform: The Prohibition Movement in the United States, 1890–1913* (Westport, CT: Greenwood Press, 1985) and Kerr, *Organized for Prohibition*.
8. *Journal of the House of Representatives of the State of Texas*, 32nd Legislature, Regular Session, 276–77. On the election reforms, see James Aubrey Tinsley, "The Progressive Movement in Texas," Diss., University of Wisconsin, 1953, 195–214. In 1910, anticipating the controversy surrounding the 1911 vote and responding to requests from around the state, State Attorney General Jewel P. Lightfoot's office published a lengthy annotated edition of the Terrell Election Law. See Lightfoot, *The Terrell Election Law with Annotations from the Decisions of the Courts and Opinions of the Attorney General's Department* (Austin, TX: Von Boeckmann-Jones Co., 1910).
9. Department of Commerce, Bureau of the Census, Bulletin 142, *Religious Bodies, 1916* (Washington, D.C.: Government Printing Office, 1920), 142, 144. On the initial struggles of the evangelicals with the earlier dominant culture of the South, see Rhys Isaac, *Transformation of Virginia*; and more recently Heyrman, *Southern Cross*.
10. Proceedings of the Baptist General Convention of Texas (1907), 92. *Texas Christian Advocate*, July 13, 1911.
11. Readership claim appears in the *Baptist Standard*, Sept. 14, 1911.
12. *Baptist Standard*, July 13, 1911.
13. *Baptist Standard*, April 13 and 20, 1911; Aug. 10, 1911; June 15, 1911.
14. Ibid., July 2, 1911.
15. Ibid., April 6, 1911.
16. Ibid., April 20, 1911; June 15, 1911; April 20, 1911.
17. Ibid., Feb. 23, 1911; May 18, 1911, p. 13 and 8; June 8, 1911.
18. Ibid., May 11, 1911; June 15, 1911; July 6, 1911; May 18, 1911.

19. Ibid., April 6, 1911.
20. Ibid., May 11, 1911; Sept. 14, 1911; Feb. 23, 1911; April 13, 1911.
21. Ibid., March 16, 1911; July 13, 1911; Feb. 2, 1911; June 15, 1911. For a detailed account of the alignment of the prohibitionist and progressive wings of the Democratic Party, see Gould, *Progressives and Prohibitionists*.
22. Jones' article was printed in both the *Baptist Standard*, June 29, 1911, and the *Texas Christian Advocate*, June 29, 1911.
23. *Baptist Standard*, April 20, 1911; March 16, 1911.
24. *Baptist Standard*, June 29, 1911; Feb. 16, 1911; July 13, 1911; Feb. 16, 1911; April 20, 1911; June 8, 1911.
25. Ibid., April 13, 1911; July 13 and 27, 1911.
26. Ibid., June 15, 1911; *Home and State*, Jan. 14, 1911; *Baptist Standard*, Jan. 5, 1911.
27. *Baptist Standard*, Jan. 5, 1911.
28. Ibid., July 13, 1911; June 22, 1911.
29. Ibid., July 13, 1911; July 20, 1911; Jan. 5, 1911.
30. Ibid., Jan. 19, 1911.
31. Ibid., Jan. 19, 1911; July 20, 1911; Jan. 5, 1911.
32. Ibid, July 27, 1911; July 6, 1911; July 27, 1911.
33. McKay, *Texas Politics*, 50; *Baptist Standard*, Aug. 24, 1911; Oct. 19, 1911; *Home and State*, July 29, 1911. A statistical analysis of the 1911 vote would be more difficult and would be less conclusive than the analysis of the 1887 vote. The variables employed, particularly county-level aggregate data on nativity, are not readily available in machine-readable form. Moreover, the lower voter turnout in 1911 would make less reliable conclusions regarding voting patterns among various Texans. Given these obstacles I have chosen not to undertake this analysis in the present study.
34. Austin *Statesman*, July 2, 1911; San Antonio *Daily Express*, July 2 11, and 14, 1887. Statewide Prohibition Amendment Association President Thomas Ball rejected an offer from Clara Murray of the Austin WCTU for assistance in establishing a daily prohibitionist newspaper, citing lack of funds for such an undertaking. He indicated his appreciation for her work in the field, and concluded that "much of the success that I believe will be ours will be due to the efforts of the women of our State," but his organization made little use of their abilities (Thomas Ball to Clara N. Murray, March 10, 1911, Clara Murray Papers, Center for American History, University of Texas at Austin). Ivy, *Rum on the Run*, 51. The Texas WCTU also became increasingly irrelevant to women working for a political voice in the state. See McArthur, *Creating the New Woman*, 116–19.
35. On the Anti-Saloon League, see Kerr, *Organized for Prohibition*, and Gould, *Progressives and Prohibitionists*.
36. *Texas Christian Advocate*, July 13, 1911; *Home and State*, Sept. 9, 1911.

Index

Aeneid 84
African Americans 2, 7, 9, 22, 27, 29–30, 32, 33, 37, 39, 41, 47, 48, 59–63, 73, 77–78, 80–81, 83, 92, 93–96, 97, 104, 105–6, 114–18
African Methodist Episcopal Church 61, 73–74
Alamo 74, 84, 103
Allen, John 20
Anderson County 25, 42
Anderson, J.M. 29
Anderson, Mac 64
Anglo-Texans 13, 23
Anti-Saloon League 2, 104, 105, 106, 107, 108, 109, 112, 119
Atlanta, Texas 54
Austin Typographical Union 64
Austin, Stephen F. 85
Austin, Texas 12, 14, 15–16
Bailey, Rev. J.W. 115–16
Baines, George 13
Ball, Thomas H. 109, 110, 116–17, 118
Band of Hope 15, 17
Baptist Church(es) 21, 31, 51, 52, 71, 91, 107, 108, 110
  See also Primitive Baptist Church
barbecue 39–40, 67–68
Baylor University 104
Beauchamp, Jenny Bland 49, 63, 100–1
beer 14, 63, 89, 92, 99, 113
Bexar County 13
  See also San Antonio, Texas
bonfires 41, 67, 90
Bosqueville, Texas 32
Bowie, David 84
Bowman, Thornton Hardie 12

Brackenridge, George W. 14
Breeding, Enoch 57
Brenham, Texas 16, 67
Briggs, George W. 16, 36, 42, 56, 57
Broaddus, A.S. 54
Brooker, W.H. 73, 75
Brownwood, Texas 67
Buckner, Robert C. 21
Burgin, P.J. 73
Burleson, Rufus 26, 27, 84–86, 87
Busch, Adolphus 113
Caldwell, Texas 89
Callaghan, Bryan 73, 79
Camp County 42
Campbell, Thomas 118
Carpetbaggers 4, 37, 55, 62, 72, 117
Carroll, Benajah Harvey 21, 31–32, 37–39, 40, 41, 42, 47–49, 51, 52–54, 57, 61–62, 67, 84, 85, 100, 108, 110
Catholics 51, 63, 97, 105, 107, 108, 113–14
Chapin, Sallie 13, 49, 60
Church of Christ 51, 52
Clark, George 33, 40, 90
Clarksville, Texas 10
Clergy 82–83, 110–11
Cloverdale, Texas 51
Cochran, Archelaus M. 97
Coke, Richard 26, 33–34, 35, 38, 39, 40–41, 42, 55, 66, 99
Collin County 42
Colored Pastors' Association of Galveston 115
Colquitt, Oscar B. 109–10, 112, 118
Compere, W.T. 51
Corsicana, Texas 91
Cotton Congress 64

147

Index

Cotton Gin, Texas 27
Cox, Carrie 48
Crain, William 63
Cranfill, James B. 22, 27, 28, 48, 55, 56, 57, 62–63, 82–83, 109, 117–18
Crockett, David 84
Crockett, Texas 67
Cuero, Texas 67
Cumberland Presbyterian Church 10
Dallas County Prohibition Convention 80
Dallas, Texas 12, 52, 53, 60, 64, 91, 104, 110
Davis, Jefferson 91, 98–99
Democratic Party 4, 9, 19–20, 22–23, 28, 29, 32, 34–37, 39, 41, 43, 53, 65–66, 69, 97–100, 112
Denison, Texas 11–12, 21
Dickinson, Susannah 84
Dohoney, Eben L. 1–2, 4, 10, 20, 22, 97
Dow, Neal 46
druggists 58, 68
Du Bose, H.M. 80–81
Dyer, John 30
Eighteenth Amendment 118
El Paso, Texas 89
Ellis County 25
Erwin, J.W. 54
Falls County 42
Farmers' Alliance 9, 19, 64–65
Ferguson, I.W. 60
Finch, John B. 55
Fort Worth, Texas 12, 35, 67, 98, 104, 109, 115
Franklin, Texas 67
Galveston, Texas 16, 63, 67, 89–90, 112
Gambrell, J.H. 108–9, 119
Gambrell, James B. 108, 110–12, 115, 117
Gambrell, Roderick Dhu 81, 87
Georgetown, Texas 12, 103
Gerald, G.B. 32

German-Texans 13, 14, 48, 63, 73, 79, 91, 92, 94–97, 104, 105, 107, 113
Gibbs, Barnett 34, 35, 52, 55, 60, 65, 66
Glen Lea Saloon 91
Gordon, Anna 7, 10, 12, 14–16
Grant, Abraham 48
Grayson County 11, 25, 42
Greenback Party 1, 9, 19, 37
Griswold, Mrs. J.T. 118
Grubbs, V.W. 57
Hale, Fred 108, 110–12, 114
Hanks, R.T. 57
Hathaway, Mary S. 12–13
Hayden, S.A. 51, 56, 57, 69, 86, 87, 98
Haygood, Atticus 62–63
Hays County 67
Hempstead, Texas 42–43
Heofling, William 13
Hill County 25, 42
Hogg, James 90
Holt, A.J. 51
Homan, William 36
Home Protection Ballot 7
honor 32, 33, 37, 42, 50, 59, 71–87, 101, 119
honor, collective 83–84
Horner, Annie 49
Houston, Sam 67, 84–85
Houston, Texas 16, 52, 104, 109
immigrants 92, 113–14
International Order of Good Templars 27
Ireland, John 66
Ivy, H.A. 118
Jackson, A.F. 73
Jasper County 65
Jefferson, Texas 10
Johns, P.W. 79
Jones, Sam 26
Jones, T.N. 112
Jones, Wash 19

Jones, Wiley 39
Kampmann, Gus 82
Kileen, Texas 67
Kimbrough, Cora 27
Lamar County 10, 51, 65
Leon County 42
Lewis, Nat 73
Limestone County 25, 65
Liquor Dealers' Association of America 53, 99, 114
local option 12, 17–18, 25–43, 45, 64, 65
Local Option Saloon 18
Lockwood, Arthur 74
Lubbock, Francis Richard 98–99
lynching 80–81, 114–15, 116
Madison County 42
Mahone, William 19
Marshall, Texas 7, 10, 18
Mathie, D. 48
Maverick, Sam 14
Maxey, Samuel Bell 54, 66
McDonald, Bill 83
McKinney, Texas 12, 13
McLennan County 25–43, 45, 66
Methodist Episcopal Church(es) 11, 20
Methodist Episcopal Church(es), South 11, 13–14, 16, 31, 51, 52, 71, 107, 108
Methodist Women's Home Missionary Society 118
Mexican-Americans
  See Tejanos
Milam County 42
Miller, Joel 54
Mills, Roger Q. 34, 35, 39, 40, 54, 59, 66, 67, 91
Moody, Dwight L. 7
Moore, James 28
Mouzon, E. D. 108
Nacogdoches, Texas 103
National Association of Wholesale Liquor Dealers 55

Navarro County 25, 42, 92
Negro Statewide Prohibition Association 115
New Braunfels, Texas 91
Palestine, Texas 67
Palmer, Annie M. 49
parade(s) 43, 67, 68, 90, 91, 103
Paris, Texas 10, 11, 12
Penn, W.E. 57
personal liberty 33–35, 38, 54, 59, 74, 78–79, 98
Pickett, L.L. 57
poll tax 105, 106
Prendergast, D.M. 48
Presbyterian Church(es) 52
  See also Cumberland Presbyterian Church
Primitive Baptists 51
Prohibition Party 1, 27, 28, 36, 55, 66, 112
Pugh, Fannie Rees 49, 64
Rayner, John B. 61–62
Reagan, John 34–35, 66, 99
Reasoner, Calvin 55, 57
Red River County 42
Reed, William 29
Republican Party 4, 19–20, 28, 32, 37, 69, 89, 97–98, 112–13
Riley, B.F. 85
Roberts, Oran 12
Rockwall County 65
Roman Catholics 107, 108, 113–14
Roosevelt, Theodore 113
Ross, Lawrence "Sul" 33, 34, 35, 38, 47, 57, 66, 67, 97
Rusk County 92
Saloon(s) 12, 13, 18, 74
San Antonio, Texas 12, 13–14, 63, 64, 67, 68, 71–76, 91, 103–4
San Marcos, Texas 67
Seelas, M. 75
Shardein, Philip 73
Shepperd, Texas 67
Sherman, Texas 10, 11, 68

Smith County   25, 42
Smith, Emma Pow   49
Southern Methodist University   104
Southwestern Theological Seminary   104
St. John, John   19
St. Louis, Missouri   56
State Prohibition Executive Committee   47, 48, 50, 54, 84, 91, 100
Statewide Prohibition Amendment Association   107, 110, 115–16
Statewide Prohibition Campaign Committee   107, 109, 118
Stevenson, James   75
Street, J.K.   57
Suffrage, female   20
Sutherland, A.H.   74–75, 77–78, 81, 82, 84, 87
Swain, William   35
Swope, Tom   109
Taft, William Howard   113
Tarrant County   25, 65
Tejanos   13, 63–64, 83, 89, 92, 94–97, 104, 105, 106, 113, 114, 116
Terrell Election Law   106
Texarkana, Texas   7
Texas Anti-Saloon League
   See Anti-Saloon League
Texas Revolution   84
Thornton, Texas   27
Towers, Laura   27
Travis County   15
Travis, William B.   84
True Blues   57, 66, 97

Truett, George   110–11
Turner, Henry McNeal   61, 73–74, 77–78, 83
United Friends of Temperance (UFT)   9, 26–28, 36
United States Brewers Association   55
Van Zandt County   42
Waco University   26, 32
Waco, Texas   12, 26–43, 47, 65, 67, 68, 90, 91, 99
Wade, Melvin   60
Waxahachie, Texas   19, 59
West, E.P.   110
West, Robert   50, 55
whisky   18, 28, 29, 30, 31, 43, 52, 57, 58, 63, 64, 72, 81, 86, 98, 99, 103, 110, 111, 113, 115
Whitten, Martha   86
Willard, Frances E.   1–2, 4, 7–23, 28, 31
Willard, Texas   49
Willis, Texas   68
wine   18, 60
Wittenmeyer, Annie   7, 8
Wolters, Jacob   118
Woman's Christian Temperance Union (WCTU)   1, 7–23, 28, 31, 47, 48, 49–50, 51–52, 56–57, 60, 63, 64, 68, 89–90, 100–1, 118
Woman's Crusade   7
Wooten, J.K.   103–4
Worrell, A.S.   51
Young Ladies' Union   17, 31
Young Men's Christian Association (YMCA)   109–10
Young, John   75
Younge, James   9, 27

www.ingramcontent.com/pod-product-compliance
Lightning Source LLC
Chambersburg PA
CBHW030345240426
43661CB00052B/1746